BRIT ABROAD

How to survive a Year Abroad

Abigail Nobes

To all of the amazing people I met on my Year Abroad

Who made my year a great one!

Brit Abroad

Copyright © Abigail Nobes, 2018

abigailnobesbooks@gmail.com

Table of Contents

Introduction

Dear Readers,

This book is designed for people going on their Year Abroad as part of their university course. A Year Abroad can be a very daunting and exciting prospect; you're going to live in a foreign country where they have a different culture, a different language and all of this can throw up a lot of different challenges. Therefore, it can be difficult to know exactly what you should or shouldn't do in order to make the most of your time abroad and get along with the people you meet. Suffice to say the challenges you encounter on a Year Abroad are varied: some of these challenges can be very exciting, for instance things like living on your own for the very first time; whereas other parts like trying to understand people and make yourself understood or knowing how to act in a professional environment with work colleagues can be a bit harder.

My one piece of advice for anyone who is offered the opportunity to study and work abroad is: Go for it! You might be nervous or thinking, I can't do this, this isn't for me, which is only natural, I felt exactly the same but at the end of the day it is definitely worth it!

Firstly, you learn a lot of new skills like, how to be flexible or adapt to new things, like cooking for example. I spent the whole year without an oven and seriously you really do learn how to adapt your cooking when you don't have an oven! And also, it makes you more open as a person, more willing to understand people's different opinions and generally you become less judgemental. I say this because on a Year Abroad you meet a lot of different people, all from different backgrounds and you also learn a lot about people's cultures which in turn makes you more accepting. Secondly, you (hopefully) have an amazing experience, you improve your language skills, make new friends, experience new things- be it new foods, new places. It is a lot of fun! And thirdly and lastly, I personally found that my Year Abroad gave me more confidence. You will grow up a lot on your Year Abroad, living alone in general helps you grow up, but living alone abroad, without anybody else around to help you, a whole different country and language, really makes you grow up. And then after your Year Abroad, when you return home you have a sense of pride and achievement, and you feel as if the world is your oyster, that you can do anything. But anyway, I digress...

In the first section of this book I recount my Spanish adventures in Ronda, where I worked as a translator for the language school *Escuela Entrelenguas*. This was my first time living alone and living abroad and I can honestly say that it is a time I'll never forget.

In the second half of the book I will tell you about my time in Tours, France. I was studying at the university, so it was a completely different experience to working in Spain. I still had a wonderful experience and it was lovely to have two such different parts of my Year Abroad.

Then I will conclude this book with a handy FAQ's, hints and advice section, which will hopefully answer any of your worries or uncertainties regarding the Year Abroad.

I hope you find the contents of this book useful, and as always, Happy Travels! ⏎

Abigail

Part 1: Spain

Chapter 1: The Arrival

What did I expect? I don't know what I expected really? I was nervous, but I hadn't really formed any expectations. They always say it's best not to have expectations, so I suppose it was good not to expect anything. But still, my experience abroad was *so* not what I expected.

The night before I went to Spain I remember praying that my flight would be cancelled, that the company I'd be working for would turn around and say: "Sorry we don't want you". But obviously that didn't happen and before I knew it I was sat on a plane from Bournemouth to Malaga.

My first time travelling by plane on my own. A big step. An adventure some may say. I was petrified. This is not an Abi thing, Abi does not just hop on a plane to Spain, to go and work there for 4 months. Abi likes holidays and visiting new places but upping her whole life and moving it someplace else, that was just mental. Abi stays at home in the evenings and watches TV, she likes a simple life, in the countryside, quiet and unknown. At least she did before...

I woke up at 4am, because we had to leave the house by 5. I flew from Bournemouth Airport to Malaga Airport. As somebody who hasn't flown in about 5 years, the flight was interesting. The last time I flew, online check-in did not exist, so that was different.

It was the first time I'd ever flown on my own which was a bit daunting. Travelling on your own is difficult, especially when ordering food. As I knew I probably wouldn't get a proper English breakfast for the next 4 months I decided to use up my time waiting for the plane in the Wetherspoons, a goodbye England breakfast. The issue with Wetherspoons is that you order at the bar and you have to give your table number. Normally this is no problem.

I said "Oh, table 5," as I'd cleverly checked that the table was free when I ordered. Very clever, I thought, there is no flaw in my plan.

But when I turned around, someone was sat there...

So, I ended up having to change the table number on the order! I was still in England and things were going wrong! Was there any hope for me surviving this Year Abroad? But it all worked out in the end, I got my food ok, so it was all fine!

The flight was boring, the lady next to me slept the whole way so I had nobody to talk to. It was rubbish. I talk when I'm nervous. I talk 24/7 anyway, but when I'm nervous it's a whole new level!

After two hours watching my pulse steadily rise from 92 to 150: my Fitbit told me I was doing cardio exercise, hahaha and staring out the window with anxious boredom we landed in Malaga... I was actually here. I was actually doing this! The journey was fine I guess, very hot but fine. The only scary bit was landing: the plane practically bounced onto the runway and then the pilot braked so hard you could hear it screeching to a halt.

Off I hopped, through security, suitcase, check. All nice and quick. I wandered out through arrivals searching around, a million taxi guys in suits, holding up signs. Where was he? My landlord was meeting me here.

Then all of a sudden, the most typically looking Spanish guy, black hair, brown eyes approached me and started kissing my cheeks.

Culture shock no 1: Some weird dude I didn't know was kissing me... well not actually kissing me but touching cheeks. Ew. Trying not to show my repulsion I kept my head still like the awkward English person I am and tried to smile. "Hola."

"Buenas, ¿qué tal el viaje?" *How was the trip?*

"Great."

After not talking for 3 hours I had to maintain conversation in Spanish for an hour and a half with my landlord, as he drove me to my accommodation in Ronda. It was lovely of him to offer me a lift but after not speaking much Spanish since May, mixed with the Andalusian accent, it was certainly a challenge.

After I'd settled into my accommodation I went out for dinner. It was only 4pm, but I hadn't eaten since breakfast, so I was starving. I went to the first restaurant I could find. It was all tapas and I was starving, so I ordered the biggest dish on the menu in hopes that it'd fill me up.

It was a big plate of scrambled eggs with jamón, mushrooms, green beans and other vegetables. It was very salty. I only managed to eat it all because I was so hungry.

Then this guy at the bar started flirting with me…I was too tired for this. Politely saying goodbye, I left, went back to my accommodation and cried.

It can be very overwhelming…feelings of "What am I even doing here?"

You're all alone, in a foreign country where you don't know anyone. You have no friends and no family. It can be quite overwhelming to begin with. And after a full day of travelling, I was exhausted. So, I had a good cry.

I had arrived on a Friday, which meant I had the weekend to explore before I began work on the Monday. The first weekend was weird, I wanted to get out and explore, but it felt funny because I was all alone.

I have always been a fairly independent person, so being on my own wasn't too bad, but I think it's the fact that you know that you don't know anybody at all. At least back home in England you know people, here I was alone.

I felt a lot fresher on the Saturday, so off I went. First thing first I had to find my place of work. I'd calculated that it'd be about a 25 minute walk away...

But before I get into that, let me actually explain where I am. I am in a small village called Ronda in Andalusia, the South of Spain. It's about 1hr and a half drive from Malaga. It is most famous for its bridge: El Puente Nuevo (the new Bridge) and the valley. It is one of the 'white villages' as all of the houses here were painted white and it's quite popular with tourists. (which surprised me as I'd never heard of Ronda before!) Just a short walk down the main street Calle La Bola and you'll probably hear at least 1 Brit, 1 French person and a German (oh and a lot of Spaniards!)

My first weekend in Ronda was good. The first thing I did was locate Entrelenguas, which I found fairly easily. Then I decided to get some more groceries. The Maskom that I'd found on my first day was very small and I'd heard there was a larger supermarket called Mercadona, so I went (vainly) in search of that supermarket.

As you can probably guess, I got lost.

I ended up walking in circles for about an hour in the heat and still didn't find the Mercadona. Eventually I gave up and headed home for lunch.

I kept myself busy that weekend, walking around the town and visiting touristy places. I couldn't believe how blue the sky was, I took so many pictures, afraid that clouds would appear at any second. Surprisingly the blue sky stayed all the way until December, but I didn't know that, did I?

I had a lovely weekend, and really enjoyed familiarising myself with Ronda, it felt like a shame though because I had nobody with me to share my experiences with. Nobody to say: "Ooh, look at that!" and have a laugh with. It didn't matter though, I thought, I'd be starting work on Monday, I'll meet more people then.

One of my most memorable experiences from that weekend was on the Sunday morning when I was wandering down the road. An old lady approached me and asked me if I knew the pharmacy opening times. I apologised and said that no I didn't know, I was new here. Unfortunately, she didn't believe me and thought I was being rude not wanting to help her. She began to shout. She didn't realise I was foreign. Scared, I caught the attention of a nearby couple and roped them into helping. Note to self: dye hair blond so people think I'm foreign.

I'm still not sure why she thought I was Spanish. I have brown hair, not black like 90% of Spaniard's and hey I didn't exactly have an Andalusian accent!

Chapter 2: Working in Ronda

Now, I'd done the clever thing of researching the company before. So, I knew there were 3 people who worked there: Mar, Alex and Javier and also Mar's dog Pongo. I wrongly assumed I was well-prepared and knew what to expect.

Assuming this, I thought I'd be the only one there, (asides from them) working at the school, so I was very surprised to see other people. There were Mari and Natalia, two of the Spanish teachers and also three other interns: Rachel, Izy and Mirco.

My first memory of Entrelenguas was when I arrived. I'd gotten there early. I started at 9, but it was about 8:40, which in Spain is unheard of. They have this thing called *'diez minutos de cortesia'* you can be up to 10 minutes late and it's culturally acceptable. Though I wasn't going to do that on my first day! Ha!

So I nervously entered Entrelenguas, not knowing what to expect and I was greeted by Javier. Javier looked like he'd walked straight off of the beach. I knew things were more casual in Spain, but I didn't realise they were this casual! He wore shorts and t-shirt and his long, black hair was still wet from his morning swim. He said hello and he casually gave me a tour of Entrelenguas, he oozed coolness, and I remember feeling very nervous. This was not at all what I expected.

But what is Entrelenguas?

Basically, Entrelenguas is a language school and cultural hub. They run Spanish lessons for foreigners living in Spain and tourists who go to Ronda on holiday. And they also run trips for tourists which include anything from tours of the town to cooking lessons in the vineyard.

My first week working at Entrelenguas felt quite slow, I was still settling in and so they weren't bombarding me with too much work. I remember at the end of my first day, going out for tapas with Rachel, Izy, Mari, Natalia and Mirco and it felt so strange going out with people and speaking Spanish. Especially after working, I felt so tired.

It can be very draining for the first few weeks as you adapt to speaking and thinking in another language and I felt that to begin with I wasn't Abi, I was this quieter person, because my brain still wasn't working fast enough to comprehend everything and work out an appropriate response.

I think what helped me settle in the most was the trip to Cadiz on the Friday of my first week at work. I'd been umming and erring as to whether I should go or not, I didn't know anyone that well yet, I was ever so tired, but something told me I should go, it'd help me get to know people better. The trip was run by Entrelenguas, the company runs a lot of trips and visits to allow their students to experience different parts of Spanish culture, but in accordance with their own tourism philosophy. Slow tourism. I'd never heard of slow tourism before going to Entrelenguas and I must admit it's a clever way of experiencing a place. It's based on seeing the real destination, not just the touristy parts, so your visit is more relaxed and you feel like you really understand the people living in the place, it's the complete opposite of the whole: 'Let's run from this tourist attraction to the next sort of thing.'

So what did we do on our trip to Cadiz? Or should I say Cadi, Cadi, Cadi.

Why am I saying Cádiz 3 times? Let me explain. If you live in the outskirts of Cadiz, in the new part they say you live in Cádizfornia (like California, but in Cadiz). And then the close you get to the centre of Cadiz, the more Cadiz' you say. For instance, if you live in the very centre of Cadiz you live in Cádiz, Cádiz, Cádiz. The people that live in the bit just before the very centre live in Cádiz, Cádiz, and well you get the gist. Add the Andalucian accent and you get Cadi, Cadi, Cadi.

Cadiz is a town in the south of Spain. It's a lot more coastal, it's almost similar to Portsmouth, but with sandy beaches and a lot more sunshine! We had a guided tour of the town, and saw lots of important monuments and buildings, including the Roman theatre. Then we ate tapas for lunch, which we bought from a local market. I had empanadillas, these are basically the Spanish version of Cornish pasties, but they come in lots of varying flavours, seriously, the menu of flavours was massive! But I decided on the spicy ones, which were full of spicy beef and chillies and some chorizo, they were really tasty.

After lunch we listened to a flamenco singer, and wow, it was amazing! I'd never listened to flamenco singing before, I'd just thought it was all about the dancing so I found it amazing. Not just the singing but the whole atmosphere in the bar was unlike anything I'd seen before. Everybody was clapping their hands to the beat of the music and at the end of the song everybody shouts: Ole!

It was also a great opportunity to get to know both my colleagues and some of the students. Normally Javier and Alex run the trips, but on this occasion, Mar was in charge. Mar is lovely, very friendly and smiley, a lovely person to have as a boss, and I couldn't believe how young she is to be running Entrelenguas, I find it very inspiring.

I also got to talk to Rachel and Izy more. Rachel is French and she's from the Reunion Island, which is down near Madagascar. She showed me some pictures, and wow, it must be a stunning place to live! Izy is English like me, though I've not once spoken to her in English so far. She is from somewhere near Essex and both her and Rachel are working for Entrelenguas on their Year Abroad like me.

Then we have Mari. She seems lovely. She speaks very quickly though and has a strong Andalusian accent so I'm still struggling to understand every word she says, but it'll come with time. After being inspired by working in the UK in Boswells and doing a bit of teaching on the side, she is working for Entrelenguas as a Spanish teacher, and it's clear that she is very passionate about her job.

I also met James, Shanna and Rosa. They are in the C1 Spanish classes at Entrelenguas, and wow their Spanish is amazing, I hope that I'll soon speak as well as they do. James is Scottish and originally moved to Andalusia to be a cycle guide about 4 years ago. Since then he has been doing a number of different jobs including teaching. Shanna is Dutch and lives in Ronda with her Spanish boyfriend. Rosa is Swiss, a lover of facts and figures, particularly regarding fines, she seems very funny and full of life.

It amazes me how everyone has their own stories and reasons for being here. I never would have thought that so many people would want to move to such a small town in the middle of the Andalusian countryside. But to be honest with you, with how nice and friendly everybody seems here, it's not surprising.

After listening to the music, we went on a boat trip across to Puerto Santa María which was lovely! This was quite eventful at the time because we needed to work out where we had to buy the tickets, which involved a lot of walking up and down the coastline and working together as a team. It was a fun but exhausting day and I'm so glad I went because it really helped me settle in. My advice: make the most of any and every opportunity you can to travel and learn about the culture of the country your living in.

Chapter 3: Adapting to Spanish life

The Spanish culture isn't very different, is it? The only differences are that the weather's nicer, the people are more laid back, a little more mañana, mañana and that's about it. Right? Wrong! Nothing prepared me for the culture shock, everything was very different, and being in such as small town, I feel the culture was so much more present than it would be if I was in a city, which was great. I'd really recommend that you go somewhere small on your Year Abroad, it will give you such a different and exciting experience and it feels more genuine.

The first thing I'll mention is the Andalusian accent. I'd always thought my Spanish was pretty good. I work hard, I'd always gotten good grades, so I was fazed by the prospect of the accent. In fact, my level of Spanish, the Andalusian accent and understanding people, weren't things that had even crossed my mind.

I wouldn't say it's something horribly difficult to understand, it just takes a few weeks for your brain to understand it, as you'll hear the normal words, but with a few changes, so you've got to adjust and get used to it.

Here are 5 things to bear in mind about the Andalusian accent:

1. The speed

Andalusia is a great place, but it is also the home to the fastest Spanish speakers in Spain!

Personally, I would say that the biggest difference between learning Spanish in class and speaking in real life with real Spanish people is the speed. As unlike your teachers, in real life, Spanish speakers don't slow down, or speak any clearer so it's just something you have to get used to!

I would recommend that you listen to as much as you can before you arrive, the radio, Spanish TV programmes, series and podcasts. Anything and everything you can. Don't worry if you don't understand any of it, the more you listen to, the more you'll understand!

2. They don't say the ends of the words

This is the difference with the Andalusian accent. Most places in Spain say *'Muchas gracias'* the same way that you learn it in class. Here, no, that'd be far too easy, here they say, *'Mucha gracia'*.
Other examples include:

Goodbye- *Adios* is actually *adio*
See you later- *Hasta luego* is pronounced *hata wego*

The easiest way to accustom yourself to this is to listen out for the start and the middle of the word. Don't listen to things expecting to hear everything exactly the way that it should be, trust me, only a handful of Spaniards actually speak the 'proper Spanish' that you might've learnt at school.

3. The pronunciation of words

As I mentioned before, they don't pronounce the words exactly the same way that you learn them. This is due to the Andalusian accent, which personally (now I can understand it) I like a lot!

It's difficult to describe the accent, they basically put all of the words together and chop off the ends of the words, here are a few easy examples:

- *Soy español*- I am Spanish
With the Andalusian accent: *Soy epañol*

- *La respuesta está en la historia*- The answer is in the story
With the Andalusian accent: La repwetaeta en laitoreya

- *Estoy escuchando a la música*- I am listening to music

With the Andalusian accent: *Etoyecuchango ala múthica*

4. There are many different accents in Andalusia

To make it even more interesting, obviously they don't all speak exactly the same. It'd be great if they did! But no, every person has their own variation on the Andalusian accent, some speak slower, some faster, some clearer, some are completely unintelligible.

My advice: concentrate, listen as well as you can, and if you really don't understand, ask them to repeat what they said. (*¿Puedes repetir por favor? Please can you repeat.*)

5. They have their own slang

Some people refer to *Andaluz* as its own language because here they use so many words and expressions that they don't use anywhere else in Spain.

Here are some examples of Andalusian slang:

- *Tío/tía*: normally this means uncle/aunt, but here they use it to mean something more like, sweetie/darling. And they say it to everyone!
- Adding -ito onto the ends of words. This is fairly normal, in Spanish you can add -ito to a word to make it smaller. For instance: mi manito- my small hand. But here everything is -ito!

- *Ajo y agua*: this doesn't have an English equivalent, it's used as an expression of resignation, as if to say, Well, what can we do?
- *Pisha*: a slang word for girl

How do you get used to this? Well, this is one of those things that you only learn from living in Andalusia and speaking to people.

At the end of the day, yes they have an accent in Andalusia, but accents are everywhere, in Spain, England, France, everywhere. To start with you may feel like you know nothing and that you'll never understand anything, but the more you listen the more you learn, and the more you speak (and make mistakes) the more you'll improve.

Personally, looking back throughout my stay, my favourite accent was Mari's accent. She's from a small village near Cadiz and I don't think I ever heard her pronounce an 's' in the whole time I've known her!

My second struggle was thinking in Spanish. I would spend the mornings from 9 until 1pm at work, then I'd go home for lunch, and then I would do something in the afternoon, like meeting up with Rachel for ice cream or going swimming, and then often we'd meet up in the evening and do something. Which to start with was very tiring, and I'd sometimes say no to doing things just because I was so tired. When you're thinking in another language, you never have time to switch off, you have to be active all the time, listening, taking in that information, coming up with a response. It takes more energy than you think. But it's worth it afterwards, when you get towards the middle or end of your stay and you feel like you don't even need to think in order to switch languages, and it just comes naturally because you've been doing it everyday for months.

Luckily, the Spanish have developed a solution to this. It's called the siesta, a small sleep in the afternoon that will rejuvenate you so you can carry on speaking Spanish until midnight! One of the biggest differences between Spain and England is the siesta. Siesta means 'nap' it is a little sleep that you have in the hottest hours of the day.

Most people think that there is only one siesta, however this isn't exactly correct, there are in fact two siestas: the first from 2pm-5pm. In this first siesta most shops and businesses close and people tend to have lunch in the restaurants and bars, and traditionally people have a small rest or sleep. As all the restaurants and bars are open during this first siesta they have their own second siesta, from 4pm until about 8pm.

But why do Spanish people have a siesta?

The main reason is so they don't have to work in the hottest hours of the day. In Spain, the hottest time of the day is the mid-afternoon, traditionally farmers and workers had a siesta in this time to shelter from the heat, but also so afterwards they feel much more refreshed and are able to work a lot longer into the evening. Because of this working hours are very different in Spain, most people start work at about 9am, they have a siesta in the afternoon, and generally work through until 7pm.

Another reason is so they can enjoy a long lunch break. Food is a very social aspect of Spanish culture, many Spaniards eat lunch together and enjoy each other's company. So, at lunch time everyone will go back home to spend time as a family, and the meal can last up to 2 hours, if not longer.

And finally, because it's good for you! Apparently, according to the experts, a nap in the afternoon is good for you. A 25-minute nap can reduce stress and increase your memory.

What do you think? Do you like the idea of having a siesta?
Personally, I thought the idea of it was great, but unfortunately, I only managed two siestas in my whole time in Spain. Sometimes I'd just be too busy, but most of the time I wasn't tired enough and it's hard to make yourself sleep during the day when you're not used to it.

As I previously mentioned, the weather is a lot nicer here in Spain. In October it was still about 27 degrees most days and even in December it only went down to 17 degrees during the day and 7 degrees at night. Throughout my stay practically every day was glorious sunshine and blue skies, it got to the point that I began to count how many days of rain we had. In the whole 4 months we had 7 days of rain. Coming from the UK, that was almost impossible to believe at first, but hey, when it rained in Ronda, it rained.

Often on the rainy days the whole town would flood. I remember on one of these days I was walking home from work with Mari. We both had our umbrellas and waterproof coats on, but they were no match for the rain. The streets had flooded up to about ankle height, so the half an hour walk home felt more like a swim or a wade home! I was so wet when I got home!

One thing you learn on a Year Abroad is to expect the unexpected. You become a lot more grown-up and flexible, as you learn to adapt to different problems and situations as they arise.

One such situation that is always fresh in my mind is when I had to get my glasses fixed. I remember I just woke up one morning and the stem was so bendy, the screw had come loose. After my vain attempts at tightening it with a knife, I realised I'd have to go into the Spanish opticians.

Normally, in the UK, I'd think nothing of this, but being abroad even a simple visit to the opticians feels like a challenge. I made sure I went prepared, I'd learnt the words for 'screw', 'loose' and 'tighten' just in case- they aren't exactly words that you learn in class.

The funny thing was, last year I was sat in a seminar at uni, listening to Miguel go on about how important it is to take a spare pair of glasses with you, just in case something happens to your glasses. I thought, 'Ok, whatever, that won't happen to me.' How wrong was I! Luckily for me, I followed Miguel's advice and took my old, spare pair of glasses with me.

There wasn't really a big problem with my glasses, it was just one of the stems was super wobbly because the screw had broken. But if I'd left it, the whole stem could've come off.

So off I went in search of an opticians. We don't have many opticians in England, but in Spain (or Ronda anyway) there are about 10 of them! So, I had the pick of the bunch. It wasn't difficult actually, much to my surprise, I just went in, explained the problem, sat awkwardly and blindly on a chair while they fixed my glasses and then bob's your uncle, sorted! And I didn't have to pay anything.

So if like me you are nervous about having to go to the opticians in a foreign country, there's really nothing to worry about. But the moral of the story: listen to Miguel, take a spare pair with you just in case! :)

With my glasses sorted, I began to notice a trend. All of the Spaniards seem to have nice shoes, in fact I would say that in Spain there is a shoe culture. Everyone always has nice, new, shiny shoes, and if that wasn't enough there are loads of shoe shops here too!

Yes, in England people wear shoes (people wear shoes everywhere), but not in the same way that people wear shoes in Spain. In Spain, a person can be dressed really casually but still have really formal shoes. Because of this it's actually really interesting to look at people's feet and their shoes. And to be perfectly honest with you, so far, I don't think I've seen a single Spanish person who doesn't have cool shoes.

Also, it's worth mentioning the shoes that the Spanish women wear. Ronda is a town with many cobbled streets, practically the whole place is cobbled, so you need to have practical shoes. Despite this, the shoes that Spanish women wear are not like this, in fact they're the exact opposite. All the Spanish women seem to wear very high heeled and impractical footwear. I don't understand how they manage it!

On my first few days in Ronda I wore my sandals, they are very practical sandals. But even for me in my practical sandals it was difficult because there are so many hilly bits and cobbles that walking through Ronda it can be quite slippery. Now, I have gotten used to it, and I can wear my sandals without a problem, but I wouldn't even attempt to wear heels!

I can't claim to fully understand this shoe culture, or why shoes are so important here. I have only realised that shoes seem to be something fundamental to Spanish culture and people judge each other on their footwear. As a foreigner, I find this very interesting, and now I'll make sure I'm always wearing nice shoes!

Chapter 4: Cooking and eating

Cooking and eating are important parts of being abroad. Everybody needs to eat, and cooking in another country can be very different.

Firstly, you have the ingredients. This isn't really something I'd thought about before, but they don't sell the same things in Spain as they do in the UK supermarkets. My advice: be flexible. If they don't have something in particular, swap it for something else. I'm a big fan of chilli con carne and to my surprise the closest thing I could buy to chilli powder was paprika, which is not as spicy, it gives your chilli more of a smoky flavour.

Secondly, I found the whole of my Year Abroad an interesting challenge as I didn't have an oven. In Spain I had a hob and microwave, and in France I only had a hob. This makes a surprisingly big difference, and I now have a very large repertoire of hob recipes! I remember when I came home for Christmas, my Mum asked me what I wanted for my first meal back home and I replied: "Anything, as long as it's cooked in an oven!"

The last thing I shall mention here is being flexible. I would often cook my toast in a frying pan and boil my water in a saucepan for my tea, as I had no toaster and no kettle.

Despite this, the most important thing is making the most of the local cuisine, and with the help of my friends at Entrelenguas and the cheap price of bars and restaurants, (one of them, El Lechuguita is 80 cents per tapas!), I did just that!

Chapter 5: Tapas

So much happened in my first month in Spain. I adapted to thinking and speaking Spanish every day, I made friends and most importantly, I learnt a lot about the culture and the food.

In my opinion, food is the most important part of the Year Abroad, and you should make the most of any opportunity to sample the local cuisine. In this case, that meant the tapas. As food is very important, I shall explain all of the yummy tapas I've tried so far.

But firstly, what exactly is tapas? Tapas is a small portion of food. The idea is you have 3 or 4 different tapas', which as a foreigner is brilliant because it means you get to try 3 or 4 different foods.

"Ensaladilla rusa"

Now to start with, I wasn't very keen on Ensaladilla Rusa, but now however, I must say that I actually quite like it. But what is it? Is it salad? No. Is it Russian salad? Well, that would be the literal translation, but no it's not really. Ensaladilla rusa is almost like potato salad, it's a mixture of onion, potato carrot, egg and tuna with mayonnaise.

It must be the most popular tapas dish in Spain, you can find it almost everywhere here in Ronda. Generally, it's served with picos (mini breadsticks) or bread. It's nice but whatever you do don't do what my friend did and order a 'ración' (big portion) of it, because it's quite rich and you wouldn't be able to eat a whole pile of it!

"Croquetas de puchero"

Now my favourite tapas has to be Croquetas! They are lovely! They are made of béchamel sauce (cheesy sauce), mixed with stewed ham. Then they are fried to give them a crispy coating. They are very tasty, or as they say here in Spain: son muy ricos! Croquetas come in many flavours, I've tried the cheese and ham ones, spinach ones, mushroom ones and rabo de toro ones! Rabo de toro is like oxtail.

My favourite ones so far have been the oxtail ones!

"Salmorejo"

Salmorejo is a cold tomato soup, very similar to Gazpacho.

To start with I'll have to admit that I wasn't too keen on the idea of salmorejo. Cold tomato soup, eww! But if it's made well, it actually tastes really nice. Salmorejo is better than gazpacho because it contains ham and is often garnished with a fried egg. Yum! It's a very refreshing dish that to me, tastes of summer! :)

Octopus

Pulpo is octopus. Yes I couldn't believe it either, they eat octopus in Spain! I was a little bit uncertain about trying octopus as it just seems a strange thing to eat, but eventually I braved it and tried some. It was actually very nice. It's a bit chewy, but it tastes good! The octopus I ate was served with potato and chips.

"Churros"

A churro is a long strip of fried dough. It is a sweet dish that is often eaten for breakfast and accompanied with hot chocolate sauce. Doughnuts with chocolate sauce for breakfast? Don't mind if I do! They taste warm, crispy and sweet! The chocolate sauce is the perfect addition for the churros.

"Empanadas"

Empanadas or Empanadillas, as I mentioned before are basically the Spanish version of a Cornish pasty. In Latin America they are referred to as Empanadas, and in Spain they're called Empanadillas.

There are many different varieties of Empanada, because you can fill them with whatever you want. It can range from ham and cheese to something like spicy lamb. You can also get sweet ones, these are generally coated in sugar so it's easy to see the difference.

Empanadas are also very popular in South America, in fact, in Argentina, each region has its own traditional empanada flavour! Thought of the day: If you could pick your own empanada flavour, what would it be??

"Montaditos"

A montadito is basically a small sandwich. My favourite montadito is a serranito. This sandwich contains a pork chop, serrano ham and fried peppers, it's delicious. But you can also get other sandwiches filled with goats' cheese or salmon and cream cheese.

I think my favourite tapas experience was when I ordered a chorizo sausage. It's something that in England we prize as being 'very Spanish' but it's not really something they eat that often in Spain. But anyway, I love chorizo so I decided I'd order it. Chorizo al infierno, Chorizo from hell. I just assumed that meant it would be spicy. It didn't prepare me for what came next...

The lady put the plate in front of me and asked me to stand back from it. It was a bowl full of white liquid and above that sat my chorizo on a skewer. I frowned at her in confusion. She smiled and using a lighter she set my chorizo on fire. The liquid was alcohol. It definitely was a flaming chorizo!

Ice cream culture

Ice cream is not strictly tapas, but I had to mention it. Ice cream in Spanish is Helado, so if you are in Spain and you would like an ice cream you can say: "Un helado por favor," (they'll know you're English instantly because you've said please, but it's always best to be polite!).

Now this is just something I've noticed since I've been in Spain, you know how in England we go out for a coffee or a cup of tea, in Spain (or in Ronda) they go out for Ice Cream! How cool is that?

Why don't we do this in England? Well, it's probably due to the weather...

The ice cream is really nice here! It's almost like Italian gelato, but better! And they don't scrimp on the portion sizes either! So when you're in Spain, don't go out for a coffee, go out for ice cream!

So far I've tried Chocolate, Mint Choc Chip, Nutella, Kinder Bueno and nuts and Nutty caramel flavour.

Chapter 6: Month 1: the good, the bad and the ugly

My first month flew by, and I was stunned at how much I learnt. Here's a small overview of what I learnt, what I've enjoyed and what's driving me mad about Spain:

All the supermarkets and some shops are closed on Sundays

Because of this you need to be prepared, make sure you have everything (food wise) that you'll need for Sunday, because if your missing even just one thing, there's not a lot you can do about it. Most touristy souvenir shops are open, but generally just for the morning. But the supermarkets- closed!

They don't sell fresh milk, only UHT milk (long life milk)

I still can't quite believe this. No fresh milk at all. They have cows, and they have milk, but only long-life milk. The first time I went into the supermarket to buy my milk I was staring into the chiller cabinet for ages, searching and searching for the milk, without success. I almost asked the shop assistant where they'd put the milk! Here in Spain they don't use a lot of milk, so they don't sell a lot of milk, so it's not worth selling fresh milk that'll go out of date.

How not to be afraid of dogs

I'm not sure if it's Spain in general or just Ronda, but this place seems to be full of dogs! And I happen to be a little bit afraid of dogs. I'm fine with dogs that aren't interested in me and just want to sit and sleep. But when they start barking and trying to hug me or lick me, I don't like it, and I like every other animal, so it's typical! But I'm adjusting. I thought I'd completely overcome my fear, but then today I was in my Spanish lesson and this guy has his dog with him in the class and the dog came and licked my knees and tried to sit on my lap and I jumped up very quickly... so I'm still afraid of dogs.

If you want nice fruit, the only place you can get it from is the greengrocers. Supermarket fruit is awful.

There are 3 supermarkets in Ronda (4 if you count Aldi, but I haven't been there yet): Día, Maskom and Mercadona.

The best for meat: Día.

The best for everything else: Maskom or Mercadona.

Despite this, for fruit, they're all not that great. Out of all of them I'd say Mercadona is the best, but yesterday it took me 20 minutes to walk there (I got lost again), plus fruit in Mercadona is double the price. So this afternoon I went to the greengrocers, a shop less than a minute from where I live, called Fruta (Fruit).

It's amazing! All yummy, ripe, not mouldy, not squashed fruit and veg! I bought 4 clementines, 2 nectarines and 2 chilli peppers (I needed the chilli peppers for my dinner). I will be returning again! Even if it does mean waiting until it opens at 5.30pm.

Even though Spain are famous for oranges, they are the most expensive piece of fruit.

This is only true in the supermarkets, the greengrocers were very reasonable. But in the supermarkets the only way you can by oranges is by the kilo, and it's about 4 euros per kilo. It' not bad, but every other fruit is 1 euro 50 per kilo, and also, I don't think I could eat a whole kilo of oranges by myself.

Spanish people don't eat their dinner until 9pm

In Spain it doesn't get dark until about 9:30pm, so Spanish people tend to have their dinner between 9 and 10pm. Unfortunately for me (as I like my sleep), Spanish people never get tired. They start work at 9am, work through til 2, then have a lunch break and siesta. They return to work at 4:30 or 5 o'clock and work through until 7pm. They return home and eat dinner at 9pm. Then they sit and watch telly or chat with family and probably don't go to bed until gone midnight. Then they get up and of it all again the next day. I don't know about you, but at 9pm I'm thinking about going to sleep, at 10pm I'm in bed! I still haven't adjusted to the Spanish times, I'm eating my dinner at 6:30-7pm, which for me feels late enough, plus by that time I'm super hungry!!

Kettles do not exist in Spain (well, not really)

Yes, seriously! When I was talking to my Spanish friend Mari, she told me that she had to explain to her mum what a kettle was because she'd never heard of or used one before. Nobody here drinks tea unless they're ill. For coffee, if you mention the words 'instant coffee' they have a heart attack, they all have coffee machines. So really, they have no use for a kettle. Therefore, every time I want to make myself a cup of tea I have to boil a saucepan of water, so I'm now an expert at boiling water in a saucepan. I know the exact amount to put in to fill up my cup and exactly how long it's going to take. So if you are a tea addict like me, bring your own tea bags AND your own travel kettle

Coffee is 10 times stronger here than in the UK

Now I thought I would be used to strong coffee, my Dad makes very strong coffee, but here Wow! It's very strong. Even when you add milk it doesn't really make a lot of difference.

If you want to order coffee in Spain:

- Café solo is a normal black coffee
- Café con leche is coffee with milk. And they charge you 20-40 cents extra for the milk. So I'm currently learning to drink my coffee black.
- Zumo de naranja is orange juice.
- They also sell granitos which are like slushies, these are very nice!

Most vegetarians here still eat jamón (Ham), apparently that doesn't count as a meat??

Yes, its true, ham is not a meat here, it is an essential part of everyday food that MUST be eaten. So, if you are a veggie here you can still eat your ham.

The Countryside in Ronda

As someone who loves the countryside and has lived on a farm her whole life, I was pleased when I saw how rural Ronda is. The centre obviously is very built up, but the outskirts is all farm land and national park. It's truly beautiful. It might not be as green as England, but it beats being in a built-up city and stops me from missing home!

Flamenco Music is actually really popular!

I always knew that Flamenco Music was an important part of Spanish culture, but I never realised how popular it was in Spain. Before I went I assumed that Flamenco music was just for oldies, but how wrong was I!

Flamenco music is everywhere in Spain, I have been out of an evening twice now to different bars where people go just to listen to the flamenco music, and it sounds amazing!

If that wasn't enough, they even have a TV show dedicated to flamenco music, it's called: Yo soy del sur, (I'm from the South) and it's a little bit like X Factor just without the sob stories. Another main difference is that firstly all of the contestants sing individually then they go in groups and it finishes with everyone singing together. Then in the last minute of the programme they randomly vote someone off, as if to say, 'Oh, we've just remembered that we're actually a TV show and we need to vote someone off.' The silly thing is, the next week they get more new contestants again, so I don't know if anyone actually wins at the end or not?? :) It seems a bit weird, but the music is good.

French in Ronda

French in Ronda... what happened there, we thought you were in Spain?

There is a French school called Habla francés (Speak French) which just opened when I arrived there. So of course, in the spirit of making the most of my time abroad, off I went with my friends to the opening of a French school in Spain.

It was a lovely evening, complete with free food and French music. The funny part was speaking French in Spain. When you know two languages you have to keep them separate. It's easy to start speaking Spanish and switch to English or switch from French to English. However, switching from Spanish to French is difficult. It's almost as if you have an invisible line in your head, one side for Spanish, the other for French, because as soon as you utter; Bonjour! in Spain the conversation follows a bit like this:

Person speaks to you in French

Response: Oui, oui, por supuesto! ... (Oui= yes in French, Por supuesto= of course in Spanish)

It's difficult. To make matters even more interesting we then got invited out afterwards to have a drink with these French people. After that, my brain was completely confused.

On the plus side I won't be forgetting my French any time soon! My French teachers Claire and Marjorie would be proud!

Chapter 7: Ronda

So, I've been going on about Ronda for a while now, and I know exactly what I'm talking about, but it's just dawned on me, that none of you know what Ronda actually looks like! So I thought I'd include this chapter with some pictures of Ronda so you can see it for yourself!

The centre of Ronda is quite built-up, it reminds me of the centre of Havant a little bit, (but it's a lot nicer!). The outskirts of Ronda however, are a lot more rural.

This is the countryside of Ronda, also known as La Serranía de Ronda.

And this is the famous bridge: El Puente nuevo

Now on to the historical part of Ronda, this is the Barrio San Francisco, the neighbourhood where Entrelenguas (where I work) is located. Here is a picture of the area:

You might notice that all the buildings are white. This looks stunning against the blue skies, but unfortunately, makes everything look the same!

And now onto the city centre. I live in the city centre. There is a main high street, which is pedestrianised, this is called La Calle la Bola (or Calle Espinel, depending on who you talk to). This is where most of the shops are located. At the end of this road is a bullring. There is also a park nearby called the Alemedra.

To conclude, Ronda is a beautiful place, and to be honest with you, I'd be happy to live here forever!

Living in Ronda is unlike anywhere else I've ever lived, there's such a sense of community here. When I walk down the road to the shop, or to work I bump into at least one person I know, and they say hello to me. It's really lovely and everybody is so friendly. It's also great to have the mixture between having all the amenities such as shops and bars in close walking distance and yet at the same time you are surrounded by countryside.

One example of how tight-knit and important the community is here, was when I helped plan a Gastronomic Event with work. Ronda seems unique in its ability to include the tourists and foreigners into its community and society. I interviewed Azzam, the main coordinator of the event and then I phoned around every hotel in Ronda to ask them to invite their guests, and most of them responded saying they'll probably attend too! I was amazed. But here is what Azzam had to say when I interviewed him:

Azzam is the coordinator of the association Raíces, who work on the integration of immigrants into the community. Azzam is originally from Palestine and after many years living in other EU countries, he came and settled in Ronda in 2001. He began working with Raíces eight years ago and is talking to us today about the organisation and their gastronomic event.

What is Raíces? What does the association do?

Raíces is an association which aims for the integration of immigrants into the community of Ronda. In the association we offer FREE Spanish courses to people from Western Sahara and Morocco. We also work with a social worker from La Cruz Roja (The red cross) to provide legal advice to foreigners, if they have issues with things such as right of residency. We are quite a relaxed group, we don't have official meetings but we meet up now and then to discuss different things and plan events.

What happens at the Gastronomic event?

We have 20 cooks at the event who will each be making a traditional dish from their country. Each cook will make enough for 50 tapas portions, and each dish will cost 1 euro, so there will be plenty of food for everyone! Our cooks provide the food, Entrelenguas provides the drinks and everything for a decent price.

The atmosphere of the event with everyone chatting, eating and enjoying time together is truly incredible, and to bring together so many people from so many different backgrounds and cultures, it's a wonderful thing.

In addition to this, we have a Tombola, you can buy tickets, sold in strips of 5 tickets (1 euro per ticket). And then you'll have the opportunity to win one of 3 bottles of wine. The wines are all from Ronda, so they are very local and we have an Austrian wine producer who has hand-picked each wine himself.

We also have 3 bottles of wine as prizes for our cooks. Everyone who attends the event will get the chance to vote for their favourite dish, the top 3 favourites win a bottle of wine. It's our way of showing our appreciation of the food and saying thank you for their hard work.

Why did you decide to run a Gastronomic event?

For two main reasons, firstly I love cooking! It is one of my greatest passions, so for me an event where people from different countries share food and explain the origins of each food is a fantastic idea!

Also, the association Raíces aims for the integration of everyone in the community, therefore, for me, a food event was a no-brainer. If you cook with people and eat the food and talk together, these people won't fight together, thus the people are integrated together as a community.

So, as someone who likes cooking, what is your favourite thing to cook?

My favourite dish is one from Palestine that I ate often with my family as I was growing up. It is called Muluolchyya with rabbit. Muluolchyya is a tall vegetable, about a meter and a half tall and is very common in Palestine. They don't sell it here in Ronda, but I've started growing it here in my garden, so I can cook it for the event on Saturday!

What happens with the money raised from the event?

As this is a charity event, each year the money goes to a different organisation that helps children. We have close links with La Cruz Roja (The Red Cross) which helps us ensure that the money always goes to the charities to help the children. 2 years ago, the money helped children in Syria, last year the money went to the charity Ronda Children and this year the money will go to help children in Yemen.

Is there anything else you'd like to say?

Just that I hope people come and enjoy the event as it's for a good cause.

Speaking to Azzam was great and the whole event really made me appreciate what an impact the community has on the people of Ronda.

Talking about community, at this stage, a whole month and a half into my Spanish adventure I feel I've made some true friends. Particularly Mari, James, Rachel and Izy, but there are also many other people and we've started going hiking together on Sunday's. One Sunday we went to El Tajo Abánico, with our trusty guide James.

El Tajo Abánico literally translates as the Fan Gorge and there were loads of really cool rocks and a cave where we sat and ate our lunch! Geologically speaking, this area would have formed millions of years ago. The area is made from Sandstone and millions of years ago this area would have been full of water. This is why the rocks have big lines on them, due to the weathering and erosion millions of years ago.

We went with Alima, Selena and Stella. Stella is one of the ladies working with Habla Francés, the French language school, so it was lovely to get to know her a bit more. She'd been teaching French in South America, before moving to Ronda to help set up the school. Alima and Selena are both students at Entrelenguas. Selena decided to quit her life as an American lawyer and move to Ronda with her husband Jason. Whilst Alima left a stressful career as a chef for the relaxing Spanish life. Everyone seems to have their own back story and reasons for being here, and I love listening to them all because leaving your life and upping sticks to Spain has never been something that's ever crossed my mind.

Chapter 8: Busy bee!

October was a very exciting month and a very busy month.

Part of the reason it was so busy was because I got to take part in an intensive course with Entrelenguas. This was brilliant because it was a B2/C1 course, so it really pushed me to get myself from the B2 level to the C1 level. As it was intensive that meant 4 hours of work in the morning, from 9 until 1, popping home for lunch and a mini-siesta and then going back for my class from 4 until 8. It was a tiring few weeks.

Despite this, it felt good to be busy, I felt like I finally had a proper purpose in Entrelenguas and I was being given new tasks and more responsibility.

Two of my favourite tasks were helping on the trip to Seville and interviewing Time for T before their concert in Entrelenguas.

My trip to Seville was very unexpected. On Tuesday night at about 9:30, I found out that I would be going to Seville the very next day. As an organised person, who loves to plan everything weeks ahead, alarm bells were ringing in my head. Off to Seville for one night and I didn't even have anything packed! Nightmare! Hahaha, it was fine in the end though!

I went to Seville with work, as we had a large group of school children visiting, so we had plenty of cool and...well let's say *interesting* activities planned.

Our first activity in Seville was the one that I'd been dreading... the bike tour. On one hand, it was lovely, and a great way to see all of the different monuments and landmarks. On the other hand, before this bike ride I hadn't actually ridden a bike in about 10 years. So, I was a little bit rusty. And in hindsight, a two-hour city tour, in the heat of the midday sun (35 degrees!) might've not been the best idea!

I was also the only one in the group who fell off. But it was all fine, my legs sported some lovely brown bruises for a few weeks after, but that was the worst of the damage. I had Javier, my knight in shining armour to rescue me!

After that was lunch time!! Tapas! We ate salmorejo, pork with a spicy mayonnaise sauce, chicken with a mustard sauce and croquetas. Note: I didn't eat ALL this myself, we shared the dishes between 3 of us!

In the early evening we did a boat tour on the Río Guadaquivir which was beautiful. All the kids were half asleep, but I was up taking pictures and making the most of it! Hehe!

For dinner we went to a restaurant called No hay lugar (There's no place). And I can honestly say 'No hay lugar como no hay lugar' (There's no place like there's no place!) the food was amazing!

We stayed the night in a youth hostel and the next day we went to the Fine Arts Museum. That was quite funny because my friend and colleague Rachel loves art, and I'm not really that interested. Let's just say she taught me a lot!

After that the group went off to the airport and we made our way back to Ronda. We got back in Ronda at 17:30 and I had to go to work again at 19:00 because we had a concert at work. So it was a quick (cold) shower and a cup of coffee, to help me stay awake, and then off to help with the concert.

The cold shower was not my choice. After not having used any water for over a day, the water in my flat was taking a long time to heat up.

The concert was with a British band called Time for T. They are an indie band and their songs are actually very good.

They even have a song called Ronda, inspired by their last visit there.

So it was a very busy, exhausting, but fun few days! I had a lovely time in Seville, it is a beautiful place with lots of cool architecture, almost like Bath (but a lot hotter and sunnier!!). And if given the chance I'd definitely go back there. (It's not as cool as Ronda though!)

Chapter 9: Hello and goodbye

The end of October was full of Hello's and Goodbye's. My friend Georgia, who'd been in Ronda volunteering in a local nursery left to go back home to the UK, and we had the arrival of the Americans.

Wednesday was Georgia's last day in Ronda. She has gone back to England to prepare herself ready for her entrance exams for Oxford University, and if anyone can get into Oxford, it's Georgia! We had a lovely evening, eating tapas and having a laugh! I'll miss Georgia's constant energy, her laugh and her craziness. Good luck for your exams and we will see you soon Georgia!

The above picture is our group with the Andalusian flag, we all wrote something on the flag for her as a leaving present.

It felt like the day after Georgia left the Americans arrived. So we were sad for a bit, but then we were excited to show our new visitors around. The Americans were a family, a couple with two young children, and after being surrounded by adults for a while, it felt great to see the children and watch them mess around and enjoy Ronda.

We did quite a few different hikes with the Americans and went for tapas with them. We found out that they were travelling for a few months before they were going to move into a ranch back in the States. It was lovely to meet them and show them around Ronda. And they were also here for Halloween, which brings me onto how many festivals they seem to have here.

Halloween in Spain is not as big and popular as it is in England. Many of the children dress up and go trick or treating, but asides from that, not much happens. Instead of traditions such as Apple Bobbing, eating a donut off of a string and searching for a jelly baby in a mound of flour, they have a fayre called La Feria de las Castañas, (The chestnut fayre).

What happens at a chestnut fayre?

To be perfectly honest with you, not a lot. It was basically a queue for free chestnuts and a cup of coffee. And that was it.

However, in Spain, the day after Halloween, the 1st November, is more important. This day is called El día de los muertos (The day of the Dead). Traditionally on this day, families go out to the graveyards and clean the graves of their loved ones. Then afterwards they all eat a meal together. Because of this, 1st November is a national holiday in Spain, everything is closed. The first ever bank holiday I've had on a Wednesday!

So, what did I do on the day of the dead?

Obviously, I didn't go out and clean people's tombs. Instead we went to the house of our American friends. Everyone bought some food, I made Chilli Con Carne, Rachel took French cheese, Mari took chicken and mushroom with hummus, just to name but a few... It was a lovely evening, eating food, chatting and enjoying each other's company!

Another important cultural difference is the bank holidays. As I just mentioned, the bank holiday was on a Wednesday. In England we have our national/ bank holidays on a Monday (plus one Friday per year for Good Friday). As you can guess, it's not the same in Spain. In

Spain, each holiday has a fixed date: for example; 8th December, and the holiday will always be celebrated that day, regardless of the day of the week. Because of this, national holidays seem to fall on very random days.

Many Spaniard's do 'el puente'. El puente means bridge in Spanish, so this means they bridge the holidays together. For instance, if there's a bank holiday on a Wednesday, they don't go to work the Wednesday, Thursday, Friday, Saturday or Sunday. So they practically get a whole week off! (I reckon we should start doing this in England!)

And there's a bank holiday on Tuesday they can do el puente for the whole week! That's why Spanish people love it when National Holidays fall on a Tuesday!

Another great festival they had the week before that was the Cinema Festival.

What is a cinema fayre though?

Well, the cinema fayre was basically 3 days where the prices for the cinema tickets were really cheap: 2 euros per person!! (4 euros if you wanted to add a drink and popcorn!!)

So we went off to make the most of this! We saw a film called Toc Toc. This is a Spanish film, with Spanish actors and a Spanish director. This film was a comedy based around a group of people who had different forms of OCD: one woman had to check everything multiple times, like if she'd locked the door, etc. Another had to wash her hand all the time; one man was a hoarder; one couldn't walk on the lines on the ground and one man had Tourette's. It was very funny and had a very clever ending (don't worry, no spoilers!).

Interesting things about Spanish cinemas:

The films are ONLY on in the evenings. You can pick between 16:30; 18:30; 20:30 and 10:30. When we went to the cinema fayre, it was the first time I'd ever been to the cinema at 10:30. Then when the film finished, I looked at my watch and it was midnight!

In England, when you go to the cinema you either have sweet popcorn or salty popcorn. In Spain you either have salty popcorn or salt and butter popcorn. As someone who normally picks sweet popcorn, this was very strange for me. Then again the salt and butter one is amazing! I think I might have been converted.

Normally in England when I go to the cinema it's practically empty. In Spain it's the opposite, practically every seat in the screen was filled. What's more, because it was a comedy, every time there was a joke/ something funny, the whole cinema erupted into laughter! The atmosphere was great!

Chapter 10: Cordoba

Last weekend I went to Cordoba with Rachel and Izy. But where is it exactly?

Cordoba is just North of Ronda and Malaga. The city is lovely, and the views are amazing. We took the train from Ronda to Cordoba on the Friday evening, which unfortunately for us, was on one of the only days of rain that we've had since I've been in Spain. So there we were, sat on the train, hurtling towards Cordoba whilst outside was pitch black, thunder and lightning and rain. It felt kind of spooky.

While I'm on the topic, I must say that the trains are very good in Spain. They are on time, there are no strikes, they're good value for money and they're virtually empty!

Luckily the rain had eased off a bit by the time we arrived, but we still had to navigate an unknown city in the dark with drizzly rain.

Cleverly, (so we thought) we decided to get a taxi to our accommodation. We were about halfway when we reached a protest. Due to the protest, all of the roads were closed, so we had to leave the taxi and walk the rest of the way.

We made it to our accommodation without a problem (using Google Maps), and the AirBnB we'd booked was lovely, it even offered breakfast. Once we'd organised our things we decided to go out and explore and have dinner.

We explored the bridge and the River Guadalquivir in the dark which was beautiful because it was all lit up. Then, much to the happiness of my stomach, we ate dinner. I think I'm finally adjusting to Spanish meal times, because we ate at 10 o'clock! I think the trick is to eat a big lunch. We went to a bar called Bar Santos which is famous for its Spanish tortillas and salmorejo, as both of these dishes originate from Cordoba. The food was great but the bar was so small, it only had one table, so we ate outside on the walls of La Mezquita (the big church/mosque).

On the Saturday, we went to the big church/mosque which is called La Mezquita. The reason I describe it as a church/mosque is because although originally it was a mosque, over the years it has changed from a church to a mosque and a mosque to a church. Nowadays it's a church, and we saw someone getting married while we were there. The thing I find very interesting about La Mezquita is the mix of the two religions; you have the arches which are from the Muslims and the decorations with gold and important figures from the Christians. Together it is quite an interesting and impressive combination.

After marvelling at the architecture of the mezquita we climbed a tower, so we could see the views of Cordoba. It was stunning, and the weather was lovely in comparison to the day before.

Then we went to see the famous street of flowers. This street is lined with blue flowerpots holding all manner of flora.

After that we stopped for tapas and a coffee, and then we went and bought tickets for a show!

By this point it had started raining...so we trekked back across the city, back to our accommodation for a small siesta. Now, no matter how hard I try, I still can't have a siesta, especially not at 6pm in the evening after a cup of coffee. So the others had a siesta and I just had a rest...and another coffee. I think since I've gotten to Spain the longest siesta I've managed is about 5 minutes!!

At 8pm our show started! What show, I hear you ask? A horse and flamenco show! Very Spanish, no? I'm not that fussed when it comes to horses, but I love the flamenco dancing. But even as someone who's not exactly a horse lover, it was amazing, and I was very impressed. The horses and their riders were so very talented, and the best bit was that the horses looked well-looked after, with nice, shiny coats and well-fed. Here is a picture I took during the show:

After that we went out for dinner. We had our table booked for 10:30 in the restaurant, but the time we finished eating... it was midnight! And we were the only people left in the restaurant.

Just some of what we ate included: nettles (yes nettles!), mini empanadillas filled with tuna, oxtail croquetas, fried squid, salmorejo and patatas bravas (basically wedges with a spicy sauce).

On the Sunday we went on a free guided tour of Cordoba. It was really interesting as they took us to places we hadn't yet seen, very small places that you'd only know if you were a local. A little bit of slow tourism! After that we hopped back on the train to Ronda.

The next week felt ever so busy and it really is starting to feel like I've made myself a life here. I think it's going to be so hard to come back home. I have a job here, friends and colleagues who feel like family and I'm enjoying myself so much here. So the most important piece of advice I could give anyone going on a Year Abroad is to make the most of it.

Make the most of every moment and opportunity you get to take part in something or experience the culture. I have done so many random things during my stay in Spain so far and that's only because I've made the effort to join in and get involved.

Just in this past week, I've been to Cordoba; a 2-year-olds birthday party; gone out for hot chocolate and shopping with my friends at 8:30 at night; attended an important tourism meeting with work; gone hiking with friends; and sat in front of a fire eating jacket potatoes for dinner (not something I thought I'd do in Spain!!- yes, it's getting colder!). And many other things, but if I listed everything, we'd be here forever!

So, the most important piece of advice I can give you, is make the most of it, because the time flies by! And by making the most of it, you have lots of wonderful memories to look back on.

Chapter 11: Settling in

Once you settle in you start to learn a lot more, both linguistically and culturally.

One of the linguistic things that I was dying to learn was the slang. I was really looking forward to speaking with the local lingo.

Here's some slang I learnt during my stay:

1. They seem to have a million words for guy/girl:

You can say:

Pisha = girl

Chiquillo/a = guy/girl

Quillo/quilla = guy/ girl in Cadiz

Illo / illa = guy /girl in Seville

Tío/a = probably the most common. Not just for Auntie's/ Uncle's, it can be used for friends and random people too.

Mi arma = it should be mi alma, (my soul) but with the Andalusian accent it changes to mi arma which actually means my weapon!

2. They also like adding -ito/a to the end of everything. Grammatically speaking this makes the word smaller, here's a few examples of things I've heard:

Un chiquitito (a small bit)

Mi manito (my little hand)

Hasta lugeocito (I love this one!)

Un poquitito (a teeny bit)

3. Greetings

Now at school we all learn that Hello is Hola, but here in Andalucía nobody says ¡Hola! Most people say ¡Buenas!

4. Venga / Anda

¡Venga Hombre!
¡Andaaaa!

These exclamations are great, they seem to have a million uses. I told my friend he was invited to a party and he responded saying 'Andaaaa!'

I've also seen 'venga' used as if to say, 'Go on, get on with it!' or 'Get up and sort it out!'

And culturally, I'm learning how to cook proper Spanish food.

My Spanish friend Mari invited me round for lunch on Wednesday and we cooked... (well she cooked, and I helped a bit), a stew with chickpeas, chorizo and beans. This stew is a very traditional Spanish dish and as you can see from the picture it was really tasty and very warming, as believe it or not, it's actually starting to get cold here!

Here you have Mari's recipe

Ingredients:

Chorizo
Black pudding (optional)
Chickpeas
Onion
Peppers
Tomato

Carrot
Beans (haricot beans)
Garlic
Bay leaf
Chilli powder
Salt and Pepper

1. Dice the onion, pepper and tomato and fry them in a saucepan.
2. Meanwhile peel the garlic and the carrot, chop up the carrot (not the garlic) and pop them in a saucepan with some water.
3. Once the onion, pepper and tomato are cooked, blend them in a blender.
4. Put this mixture in a big pan and add the boiling water
5. Add salt, pepper, a bay leaf and chilli powder
6. Add the beans and chickpeas
7. Cook until the water has boiled off and you are left with a thick stew
8. Enjoy!

Chapter 12: November

November was a month of change. The weather began to get colder, well, colder inside, but still about 17-20 degrees outside, and Entrelenguas began to get quieter. Despite the change, there was still plenty going on...

Last Thursday we went to listen to the flamenco music in Las Martirios again and this time we decided to try the food too!

Las Martirios is a fish restaurant, which wouldn't normally be my first choice, however the food was great! We ordered a sharing platter of fried fish, (to be honest with you I'm not really sure what type of fish I was eating, but hey they tasted great!), mussels, a prawn stir fry (this was my favourite) and some raw tuna thing (I didn't really like that one). Oh and there were 5 of us- I didn't eat this ALL by myself!

Flamenco music is very quintessentially Spanish, particularly in the South of Spain. Flamenco was first created in Seville and its music and dances date back all the way to the 1700's, so it's a very old tradition. We went to listen to the music, which was such a different experience. To start with it feels as though the singer is just shouting, or crying, there's so much emotion that it's hard to make sense of it. But after a while, if you listen hard and carefully to the words, you become absorbed in the singer's passion and emotion- even if you don't understand every word; you understand the message. To me, flamenco music and the dancing is a show of true and pure emotion, so unlike anything I have ever seen. In England we are quite reserved and don't tend to put our feelings on the line for others to see; let alone shouting them at the top of your voice. So, to start with, this music seems a bit alien-like, we are unsure what to make of it and as a Brit we might think it sounds awful. But when you ignore your first instincts and really immerse yourself in it, it's almost quite magical. So, I would definitely recommend listening to flamenco singing especially if it's live. Flamenco is all about the emotions and the atmosphere; something you can only really experience if you're there in the room with the singer; hearing the Ole!'s of the crowd; the clapping; the guitar; it all adds up to give you the true experience of flamenco.

November was also the month of quite a few people's birthdays. And well, it's only when it's someone's birthday that you get to eat tiramisu in your Spanish lesson!

But how do Spanish people celebrate birthdays?

I was quite surprised at this, I assumed Spanish people would do different things on birthday's or have random traditions; but it's all quite similar to birthdays in England. They have birthday presents, cake, a meal out with friends/family, a party.

Considering this, there are a couple distinct differences.

1. Cake: often in England cake is cake, like Victoria Sponge, etc. In Spain birthday cake can be anything from a mountain of ice cream sandwiches to tiramisu, to an actual cake.
2. The song: obviously they don't sing the same song, there's a Spanish version. It has the same tune but with different words:

Cumpleaños feliz

Cumpleaños feliz

Te deseamos a ti

Cumpleaños feliz

3. Organisation: In England, I like to get everything ready in advance (present-wise). In Spain it's a little more Mañana, mañana! We did a group present

and had everything ready by 11pm the night before!

4. People don't seem fussed about their age: In England anyone past the age of 30 seems touchy when it comes to how old they are. In Spain it's the opposite: "Ahhhh! I'm so excited I'm going to be 32!!!!"

5. Presents: In England, normally if someone gives you socks as a present it's a bit of a naf gift. In Spain however, socks seem to be a very exciting present that are gifted to everyone!

Would you like socks for your birthday?

Chapter 13: Unexpected experiences

As always, a Year Abroad brings a host of experiences that you don't expect. These can be very small things; like culture shock or falling in love with a place you thought you'd hate; or they can be opportunities that you don't envisage.

The last week or so of November bought a few unexpected experiences, some which were more enjoyable than others; but all gave me a deeper understanding and insight into how things work in Spain; culturally but also socially.

The first of these was an opportunity with work; my boss invited me to go to a tourism meeting. This meeting included the bosses of all the other language schools in Ronda, and also the Council Ministers for Educational Tourism. This was an amazing opportunity and it was interesting from a business perspective, to watch how the other people in the meeting interacted with each other; trying not to say too much for fear of warning the other schools of their ideas or business plans and it made me realise how important tourism is for Ronda.

My second experience was a visit to the Doctors with my friend Mari. She wasn't feeling well and so I went with her, so she didn't have to go alone. Also, it was an interesting chance to experience what Spanish health care is like, without being ill myself.

As with everything else, Doctors surgeries are different in Spain. But hey differences are great, and I've been lucky to be able to experience all of this sort of thing. It makes you realise that if you were living here permanently and you did need to see a doctor, you'd know what to do and what to expect.

And from my experience, the Doctors surgeries in Spain are a whole lot nicer! For a start they're a lot more modern, and a lot bigger. This is because most of them had only been built in the 80's, after Franco's dictatorship.

And surprisingly they're even a lot quieter! We were the only ones there, whereas normally in the UK they're all packed full to the brim. Mari hadn't booked an appointment and we only had to wait 15 minutes for someone to see her, she was very lucky.

The third experience wasn't quite as nice. I went to a funeral. It wasn't exactly the funeral bit, but, let me explain how it all works in Spain.

In Spain when someone dies they must have the funeral the following day. The funeral is generally the evening of the following day. During the daytime, before the funeral, all of the family and friends of the dead person can visit to come and pay their respects and comfort the principal mourners (generally the family members who are closest to the dead person). These principal mourners have to stay at the morgue for the whole day to welcome the well-wishers and mourn. This bit is called "El tanatorio".

I only attended this bit in the morning as I didn't personally know the person who'd died, I only knew some of the family. Despite it being a sombre occasion and a sad way to end the month, I learnt a lot from it.

Chapter 14: December in Spain

December. My last month in Spain. I still can't believe how fast its all gone. I feel like I've made myself a life here; like I could stay here forever, but it's almost already time to leave.

I think my December was probably the best month. I was 100% happy and settled and I had some great travels and experiences to finish off my stay.

The first being my trip to Malaga. The guiris of Ronda went to Malaga! Guiris is a slang term (only used in the South as far as I know), which means foreigners. The day we went was a Wednesday, but it was a bank holiday to celebrate the Constitution Day in Spain. So when you don't have to work, what better thing to do than spend the day in Malaga.

This was my first time in Malaga, (asides from about an hour when I was on the aeroplane) and like many people I thought that Malaga was literally just a beach and a whole load of tourists, but I was most definitely wrong. In fact, we seemed to be the only tourists there, everybody else was local! And if that wasn't enough there's a whole host of things to do in Malaga!

As it was so close to Christmas we went to see the stunning Christmas lights. Here is a picture, which shows that they even look good during the day!

As we were wandering through the streets of Malaga we listened to a speech about Spanish constitution and being proud to be Spanish, then we popped into a cathedral to see the Belen. A Belen is a Nativity scene, and this one was very detailed, it included every single part of the Nativity Story.

Afterwards we went to see the Roman theatre and then walked up to the castle. This castle is called Castillo Gibralfaro. We had a look around the castle (there is a small museum there too) and the views from the castle were beautiful. By this point the temperature had increased dramatically, to about 25 degrees! It felt like we'd gone from winter to summer! It was such a surprise, I'd completely forgotten that Malaga would be warmer. Ronda is up in the mountains so it's quite chilly in the winter, whereas Malaga is on the coast, making it sunnier and hotter. It was lovely to make the most of the warmth and sun, even if I had come prepared with ten trillion layers! Hehe!

After descending the castle, we walked along the beach and then we stopped for lunch! Now, all this time I've been telling you about tapas or different Spanish traditional foods. Having been here for 3 months now, living off of tapas, there is a point where you don't want to eat tapas anymore. So, we went and had a burger! It was really tasty! And nice just to have something different!

Then we looked at the Christmas markets and an art/sculpture exhibition. And then it was back on the bus to Ronda!

It's strange because it reached the point where I'd return to Ronda and think, 'I'm back home now', it feels so strange to be able to think of a place in another country as home.

So for all those who think that Malaga is just a beach, tourists and foreigners, there is more there than you think and it's well worth a visit!

After the bank holiday Wednesday off… there was another bank holiday weekend, yay! This weekend, for *El puente,* the bank holiday weekend, I went to Granada to visit some of my uni friends who were studying there.

I took the train at 7:50 from Ronda to Antequera, and then a bus from Antequera to Granada. Normally they have a direct train, but they are currently doing works on the train lines near Granada. It was the first time I'd travelled on the train on my own in Spain, normally I was with friends, so on the way there I was really nervous that I'd miss my change over or get off on the wrong stop.

I arrived in Granada at 10:30 and met up with my friends Florin and Rocio. After a quick coffee we went to explore Granada. Rocio's friend Andrea was there too. He is Italian and doesn't speak much English, or Spanish or any other language. So that was interesting. We spent the whole day speaking Spanitalish: Spanish, English and Italian, a mixture of everything, as I don't speak Italian either (only about 10 words). Interestingly though, we found out that if I speak English slowly and he speaks Italian slowly we can actually understand each other. It was kind of cool to be able to understand a language when you can't speak a word of it. And I can honestly say that over the course of the weekend my Italian has improved immensely, I might even know 20 words now, hehe!

But what did I do in Granada? Rocio and Florin were my guides and they did a fab job of showing me around. Firstly, we went to a Palace which was full of Arab architecture, with all of the arches and patterns, it was really beautiful. We even went on a guided tour in Spanish.

Then we went and saw the Cathedral and the Belen. They are very popular here in Spain. It's amazing to see how much work goes into creating the models and the different scenes.

Then we stopped for lunch in a Moroccan kebab place. The food was great, even if we did wait about an hour for it because the waiter confused our order because he didn't speak any Spanish.

After our food had gone down we decided to make our way up to the Mirador, the viewpoint from which you can see the Alhambra. We went up past the Mirador, almost to the top of this hill and made the most of the beautiful views, watching the sun going down. It was stunning! And a great laugh with some great friends! I didn't realise how much I missed my friends until I saw them again!

We went out in the evening for some drinks and tapas. Most bars in Granada do a deal; whenever you order a drink you get a free, random tapas with it.

The next day, very early in the morning, Florin and I went to the Sierra Nevada! The tallest mountain in Spain and Europe, and one of the things on my bucket list!

It was an amazing experience! We went up by bus to the main area where there are bars, hotels and skiing centres. There were about a billion hairpin bends on the way up, so I was very happy to be getting off the bus!! From there we continued walking up.

We didn't go the whole way up, we were ill-prepared. Everyone was wearing special snow shoes and we had trainers, so we slipped and slid our way up the mountainside! It was very funny! We spent about an hour in the snow, building snow men and enjoying the view. Then we popped back down for a quick hot chocolate before getting the bus back to Granada.

Chapter 15: My last few days in Spain

My Spanish adventure was coming to an end! I was so sad. I was really going to miss this place, but before I left I had to make the most of my last few days. It was during these last few days that I came up with the idea of creating this book. I'd had such an amazing experience and really wanted to be able to share it with other students doing a Year Abroad, so they know not to worry and so they can feel prepared.

In my last week of work, we had a Christmas party with all of the students. This was by far my favourite event in Entrelenguas because everyone was there, and it made me realise how Entrelenguas is just like one big family for all of the foreign people living in Ronda.

The last week in Ronda was full of lasts: the last trip down to the bridge; the last hike; the last tapas and the last cake. The best 'last' thing was my last night in Ronda.

We went to James' house and Alima cooked us tandoori chicken, roast potatoes and cauliflower cheese. It was delicious! And if that wasn't enough we ate like Brits, at 7:00! Then we sat and watched the Strictly Come dancing final! It was a lovely evening and Joe won! Yay!

It's the most British I've felt and was great to help me get used to speaking English again. The food was amazing and so was the company. Alima was a catering manager when she was in the UK, so she really does know how to cook! She is lovely, she's even offered to give me a lift to the airport tomorrow.

The next morning at the airport felt strange, sitting down on the aeroplane and munching on my paté baguette, flying home for Christmas knowing I was leaving Ronda, my new friends and my new life behind. But I was happy. I had an amazing time, made the most of every single second and I have no regrets.

Chapter 16: Goodbye Spain

When I arrived in Ronda, I couldn't wait to leave again. I didn't think I'd be happy here, I didn't think I'd enjoy my time here. How wrong I was!

I have had an absolutely amazing time and met such amazing people, a special mention to my bestest friends in Ronda, *los Guiris de Ronda*, who I will miss so much! But don't worry guys, I'll be back to visit you soon! Rachel, Mari, James, Georgia and Izy! Thank you all ever so much for everything! You have made my experience here a great one! From eating tapas, to film nights and visiting new places like Cadiz, Seville, Cordoba and Malaga, I'm going to miss you all a lot! With your help, my time in Spain has been more than just 'time in Spain'. You have made me feel at home here, to the point that I feel I could stay here forever! I'm not a sentimental person, so I reckon that some of that Spanish emotion and Andalucian openness might be rubbing off on me at long last.

I have also loved every moment working with Escuela Entrelenguas, from the general tasks like translating emails and blogs to answering the telephone, to the more exciting bits like dappling in a bit of interpreting on the cooking courses to helping out with the school group in

Seville. I will remember every moment and all of the lovely, wonderful people I have met, from the staff Mar, Alex and Javier, to all of the students at Entrelenguas who have made my experience such a great one!

Thank you everyone! I will miss you all! But I will come back to visit you all as soon as I can.

So, to conclude part 1, my advice for any student doing a Year Abroad is to make the most of it. Speak the target language everyday, do things and make the most of every opportunity that comes your way! And that way you won't have any regrets!

¡Adiós Ronda y hasta pronto!

Part 2: France

Chapter 1: Goodbye England, hello Tours

Just recovered from Christmas and the New Year. As they say, no rest for the wicked! I am currently sat on the plane to Paris. Lucky ducky, some might say. I agree I am very lucky to have this experience. But it's never a piece of cake. Saying goodbye to my family again was harder than it was the time before. I'll be away for 5 months and after having been away for 4 and only being back home for 2 weeks, I feel sad leaving them again so soon. But I'm not too fussed, some things in life you just have to do. And they'll still be there when I get home. They might even visit me in France.

So, what am I worried about?

I haven't spoken a word of French (properly) since May...

Fingers crossed it'll all come flooding back to me when I land!

Hello again! This is Part 2 of my adventures. In this section I shall tell you all about my experience studying in France at l'Université François Rabelais in Tours, France. Tours is located in the Loire Valley, and is in the centre of France. Unlike Ronda, Tours is a city, about the same size as Portsmouth, and I am excited at the experiences and challenges up ahead!

I arrived in Tours on the 4th January and wow, after spending 4 months in sunny Spain, the weather has been a bit of a shock. It's so cold here! And rainy! I think this'll take some getting used to.

I remember being a lot more nervous about France than I had been about Spain. I think it was mainly as a result of two things:

Firstly, the language. I hadn't been worried at all about the level of my Spanish when I went to Spain. I think this is because my Spanish level has always been higher than my French level. I started French as a beginner when I started university, so I've only been studying it for 2 years, whereas I've been studying Spanish for about 7 years so far. Despite the fast-paced and thorough French course at my home uni, I'd never really felt as confident with my French.

Secondly, there was all of the paperwork. There are a lot of forms to fill out for studying at a foreign university, particularly for France- the French love their paperwork and bureaucracy! I remember having to fill in all these papers for the accommodation in November, whilst I was still in Spain and I wasn't 100% sure if I'd filled them all in ok. I remember being full of dread, thinking they'd turn me away and say, 'No, you can't live here, you didn't fill out the paperwork properly.' (Luckily this didn't happen though, in fact it all went swimmingly!)

But my first challenge was actually getting to Tours...

Chapter 2: My journey to Tours

My journey to Tours began at 4am on Thursday morning when I got up bright and breezy to get to the airport. Well maybe not bright and breezy, but I was awake!

I flew into Paris. A lovely, short flight- thank goodness! We were still in the aftermath of Storm Eleanor, so we couldn't remove our seatbelts for the whole flight due to turbulence and people kept throwing up. The poor little girl in front of me hadn't flown before and spent most of the flight saying to her parents: 'Get down now,' because she didn't like it.

After 50 minutes of successfully attempting not to be sick we landed. Considering that we'd left a few minutes late, we managed to land earlier than anticipated due to the powerful winds pushing us around. Lucky us!...

Now I've been to some big airports in my time, but I don't think any of them have been as big as Charles de Gaulle, its massive! We had to get a bus from the plane to the terminal! Once I'd got my case it was time to find the train station which conveniently is below the airport. So, after lugging my case (which was heavy, it contains everything I'll need to survive 5 months in France), down countless escalators I was in the train station.

The train station was really big too, and a lot busier than I'd expected considering it was a Thursday. Luckily, I managed to spot a chair and made myself comfortable while I waited for the train.

When the train finally arrived, I got on. Trains in France. What can I say about them? Trains in France are like double deckers, and I was on the top deck. Each carriage has a flight of stairs to take you up there. A flight of stairs that I had to get my case up. If that wasn't enough, on reaching the top all of the luggage racks were full, so I sat for 2 hours with my case squished at my feet.

Then the train arrived in Saint Pierre de Corps, (4km from Tours). I got off and was then challenged with the task of finding a bus to Tours. I asked a man at the information desk who spoke to me in super-fast French. I didn't understand him...at least not everything. I could get a 5, a 10 or a something bus or a train in a few hours' time, but the bus station wasn't here it was somewhere else... I got a taxi instead. The taxi was far simpler and very quick, within no time I was at my hotel.

The next day I went in search of the accommodation office to get the keys to my uni accommodation. I was very clever and decided that I would walk there, it'd only take 20 minutes...famous last words. 1 hour and two very achy arms later I finally found the office. Hahaha, I'd walked past it, twice!

Despite my adventure finding the office, everything went well there: all of my forms were fine and it all went quite smoothly. I got my key and off I went excited to be moving in. I wasn't quite as excited when I discovered I was on the top floor and I couldn't find a lift... fun and games!

The worst bit was later on when I went out to get some groceries and what did I find? The lift. I'd lugged my case up all of those flights of stairs for nothing! Oh dear! At least I know where it is now!

Chapter 3: Touring Tours

Settling in the second time round was a lot easier. I knew what to expect, how to look after myself, and generally, how to get by on my own. I was in Tours, a big city, so it was easy to find supermarkets and there were plenty of places to visit and explore.

But where exactly is Tours?

It won't come as a surprise that Tours is in France. It's located in central/North Western France, about an hour and a half from Paris. Tours is part of the Centre-Val de Loire department; the capital of this region is Orléans.

I would say that Tours is the size of Portsmouth or Malaga, it's a big city, which felt very strange for me as I've only ever lived in small towns or villages. Tours itself is split into 3 sections: North Tours (above the Loire River), the centre (between the two rivers) and South Tours, (below the second river).

I was living in the centre of Tours, about a 30-minute walk from my uni building and about 30 minutes from the train station, so it was quite a good location.

To begin with though, everything felt quite slow. I was there two weeks before any of the lessons actually began. I had to be there to fill out forms- don't get me started on French paperwork and bureaucracy! And I didn't know anyone yet...all the other Erasmus students, who were in the same boat as myself, were still settling in and not ready to go out and get to know people yet, which was frustrating. I felt lonely for a bit, there's only so long you can spend in your own company, but I feel like I learnt an important skill from it. Enjoying my own company. Never before had I been happy to go exploring or visiting museums alone. I always preferred going with friends or family, so this felt very different. But I actually found myself enjoying it. You have such a different experience going somewhere alone. On your own you can go around at your own pace, you can go where you want to go, you don't need to think of others and also random people tend to talk to you more if your alone. I made so many old lady friends on the buses!

So, I went exploring on my own to start with; braving the cold, rainy weather and making the most of getting to grips working my way around, so I wouldn't get lost.

But what does Tours look like? As I mentioned before it's a city about the same size as Portsmouth (which for me is massive, but all the French people here are like, Oh, Tours is so small! My response, are we in the same place? It's massive here!) As with any city, there are parts that look pretty and parts that look a bit less pretty. Let's start with the city centre and Rue National. This part is the top of the Rue National where you have the bridge across the Loire River which links North Tours to Central Tours. It's very pretty, especially in the snow:

The Rue National is lined with shops, boulangeries and there's even a stall selling hot chocolate and mulled wine. The tram also runs along this road, so you have to be careful not to get run over by the tram. I was surprised about the tram because the only trams we still have in England are old and wooden. The trams here, in stark contrast are modern, shiny and new.

Then following on from that you have Place Jean Jaures where you can find the town hall and the law courts.

Another part of Tours I'd like to show you is the old part of Tours, *Vieux Tours*. It has quite a bit of character, and you can even find a square called *Place de Monstre*.

Close to this is a big building called *Les Halles*, I have no idea if 'Halles' means anything in French, but I went inside to have a look and there's loads of places selling food, like an indoor market.

Well, I hope that gives you all a good sense of what Tours looks like. Similarly to Ronda, quite a lot of the buildings here are white (well they look a tad more grey) and they have these cool dark grey slate roofs, which looks pretty when it's sunny, but when it rains everything just looks grey (like England, haha).

Chapter 4: Making French friends

Unlike my Ronda adventure, settling in hasn't been 100% straightforward, in fact I did find it hard making French friends to start with. It was difficult because I wanted to get on with it and meet people, but it felt a bit like nobody seemed to want to know me. I'll explain more below, and that, combined with the fact I was missing Ronda, made it even more challenging.

I'm a friendly person. I'm not scary and I'm not horrible, so I don't normally have trouble making friends. Despite this, making friends in France has been a challenge.

As a friendly person I automatically have a smile on my face and when I meet people I say Hello to them. I thought this was perfectly normal. I still think it is and should be normal. Though I've had some interesting experiences here so far.

I smiled at someone in my class and said Bonjour. They didn't even say bonjour back to me. They frowned and asked me why I was smiling. My response, because I'm happy. She looked at me like I was crazy, like I had some kind of problem...

Second experience: I sat down in the class. I decided to sit next to a French girl, so I could finally make a friend. She was sat all on her own, so I thought: 'Perfect I can do this.' I sat down, smiled and introduced myself. Got a one-word response of Bonjour. Tried to attempt a conversation several times. Failed. Some other people sat the other side of me, I said Bonjour to them, so did she. They then proceeded to blank me and have a conversation across me, like I wasn't even there, I was invisible...

Third funny experience: I was early to a class, so I just sat down in a seat, not bothered. Every other aisle filled up with people. Apart from my row. It was like they knew I was foreign and they didn't want to sit near me for fear of catching some sort of disease.

This is not helped by an interesting cultural difference. French people like to stare. I know it's because I'm foreign and I stick out like a sore thumb, but this has been one of the hardest things to adjust to.

I don't like to stereotype but I want to tell the truth, there's always something that's not plain sailing. If I was to lie to you this book wouldn't be a true representation of my year abroad. The French people here in Tours...they all have a particular style and that style is very similar. They tend to wear dark, plain, muted colours, black, dark purple, grey, dark blue. All very dark and very plain. No patterns and nothing multi-coloured.

I on the other hand enjoy wearing bright, clashing colours. Therefore, I have been the very lucky recipient of the French stare.

In England it's rude to stare, here not so much... at least I hope not because they all do it! So what do I do when they stare at me. I greet it with a smile, a wave and a bonjour! It makes me feel less creeped out and it seems to creep them out which I find quite funny.

But it works! Random people have started saying bonjour and salut to me around uni. I have no idea who they are, but I think I'm making progress!

Although staring seems to be part of French society I think it's one of those things I won't get used to, it'll still creep me out and make me think, "Stop staring at me you weirdo!" but it's interesting to observe what is acceptable in some cultures and not others. Here it's perfectly fine for someone to stare at you for like a minute, without smiling, almost like they're giving you evils, they're not though, they just don't seem to smile as much here. It's something we don't really do in the UK, so it feels weird to me.

Despite all of the interesting experiences and initial challenges, I have Meggy, my French friend who did an exchange at Portsmouth last year. She's lovely and she even introduced me to two of her friends this week and they were also lovely! So, it's not all French people, just some, I've just been a bit unlucky I suppose.

Also I've started doing Tandem which is like a language exchange, I met a girl called Camille on Monday who was lovely! And today I met a guy called Luke who seemed friendly too.

So my advice to any foreigner, from any country really, going to France and wanting to make friends: **Be persistent and don't give up.** You will have bad experiences, you will feel like French people hate you, but it's just part of the process of settling in and working out which ones are the nice ones and which ones don't really care and don't want to get to know you.

In hindsight I would also add that in France it takes time. All of the French people I was meeting had all known each other from the age of 9 or 10. I was a new person. Nobody knew me, and nobody wanted to know me, because they already had friends. So, I would say to anyone trying to make French friends, don't take it personally if nobody wants to know you, and as I said above, be persistent, it takes time for the French people to trust you and want to get to know you.

Chapter 5: University in France

Studying at a University in France, exactly the same as studying back at home...right?

Not quite...

I was told before that it is very different studying in France, but nothing really prepared me for HOW different it is. I've now done a whole weeks' worth of lessons and I've survived! Just about...

I don't want to be negative, so I'm just going to say that this week spent trying out lots of different courses has given me a good idea which courses I like and which ones I hate. They encourage you to try lots of different courses that first week, just in case you go to them and you don't like them, or the teacher doesn't accept you in their class- yes that is possible. So, I must admit I am very happy that I took their advice and went to as many classes as I could.

Just to give you an idea though, here are 3 big differences between studying at uni in England and France:

Organisation: this didn't really bother me much. Last term I'd heard all the horror stories from my friends about how they didn't have a timetable for the first 6 weeks and they didn't have a student card, so this wasn't a shock for me. Personally, I think it's gone quite well for me, I've only waited 1 week and a half for my student card and I have a timetable, so it's all good. But it is quite different to the UK where you get both your timetable and student card on the very first day.

Lectures and seminars: in the UK there *is* a VERY big difference between lectures and seminars. Lectures are in big room 100 people plus and they talk at you and present a topic. Seminars are normally 20 people maximum, they are more practical and more focussed (and more interesting).

Here, I've only done seminars, for that exact reason, and some of these seminars are identical to lectures. The teacher sits there and speaks at you for two hours and everyone sits writing EVERY single word the teacher says. They don't even do bullet points. It creeped me out, I was thinking, are they all robots or something? I just kept thinking: Why are they all writing so much? Should I be writing too?

A handy thing to remember:

CM = cours magistral which is a lecture
TD= travail dirigé which is a seminar

Blackboards: In France they still use blackboards, or here, 'green boards' with chalk and everything! It's like being in the Victorian era! It's kind of cool.

So after my interesting experiences the first week, what courses did I end up picking? Every university, regardless of country has different courses, so wherever you go there'll be different things on offer, so you can use this information about what I chose to help you make your own decisions.

The first thing I have to say is that after not studying since about May last year, it is very hard to get back into the studying frame of mind. But I'm getting there. The classes are fine, they keep me busy, it's just the motivation to do the homework or extra reading or going over my notes. I keep feeling like I'm on a holiday where somebody's forcing me to study!

Translation for Exchange Student Classes
I take two of these classes, the French to English and English to French translation. I like these classes. In comparison to the others they are easier to follow and understand and I've learnt a lot of new French words in these classes.

They also offer normal translation classes with the French students; however, I would encourage others to check these out before they pick them. In France they have a different system for translation: dictionaries are banned and every mistake you make = -1 mark...there's only 20 marks as it is. This means these courses are incredibly challenging and also bear in mind that they are often taught by French teachers who believe that their English is better than your own English and will tell you that you're wrong when you're right. This happened to a friend of mine.

Analyse d'oeuvres B
This is a literature course. We are studying En attendant Godot (Waiting for Godot) and Le ravissement de Lol V Stein (the happiness of Lol V Stein). It's my worst class of the week... We sit and listen to the teacher speak for 2 hours. She speaks very fast and has a very soft voice, even

with a microphone, (yes it's a seminar as well, not even a lecture in the lecture hall!)

People are supposed to be doing speaking presentations on the books (I don't have to do this as I'm an Erasmus student, I'll write an essay instead), and every week the people doing the presentations are mysteriously 'ill' so we get to listen to the teacher talk for the whole time. This week someone finally wasn't ill, so we saw a presentation...it was 5 minutes instead of 20 and after that the teacher spent the whole lesson moaning and saying how they'd get a zero. So encouraging!

Despite this, every week my notes for this class are a bit longer and a bit more detailed, so I'm improving! And it's great for listening comprehension practise! The worst part is that we have a 5-minute break between the lesson and the first half is generally great, I take lots of notes, I understand almost everything. But after the break I feel tried and bored and it all goes downhill.

Tandem
This is quite fun, I like this course because I get to speak to random people in French and then in English. The idea is that it's supposed to be 30 mins French and 30 mins English but it tends to be more like 40 minutes French 15-20 minutes in English. This is great for me as I get extra practise! And a lot easier because some of the student's English level is so low, I struggle to understand anything they say. I just smile and nod, so I don't make them feel bad!

I have met some very nice people through the tandems and have had the chance to talk about a wide range of different topics. I think it's a great way to gain confidence speaking French. One week, my tandem didn't show up, so I was paired with 5 French people, I never thought I could speak French with that many people at once, but I managed it, for an hour and a half as well! I was shattered afterwards.

Langue écrite

I like this class, it's funny! Last week I asked what un drageur means because it was in one of the texts we were reading. It's the French word for a flirter and the teacher, instead of telling me that, she decided to start flirting with me. I was very worried and confused, thinking What on Earth have I said!? And the rest of the class were in hysterics! When I finally got what she was going on about, it was quite funny. I think this class is going to be very useful as we are learning about different texts, like summaries, commentaries, dissertations and essays, how to write them and structure them in French, which will be very useful for my assessments.

Langue orale

This is my favourite class of the week, which is surprising considering it's 2-4 on a Friday afternoon. Each week we learn 5 idiomatic expressions and we do a lot of speaking. Generally, we watch a 7 to 10-minute video and then discuss it. I enjoy this class as it helps me improve what I most need to improve: my listening and speaking skills.

Littérature Jeunesse

Unfortunately, this is a lot like Analyse d'oeuvres B, however it's only 1 hour per week (8-9 on a Thursday morning: 8am lessons should be illegal!). So, it's ok and the books are all children's books so they're a lot easier to understand.

Beginners Italian

This is a fun challenge! It is difficult sometimes to work out if the teacher is speaking French or Italian, as due to my Spanish knowledge I can understand both, so it's only an issue when she asks me a question and I'm thinking: Which language did she just say that in? Should I reply in French or Italian? We've learnt so much so far which is great and I'm really enjoying learning another language!

Overall I am enjoying studying in France. I must admit I prefer studying at Portsmouth University because the classes there are more interesting, focussed and a lot more practical. However, I think I'm doing alright here, the assessments so far have been ok, but I'll know for sure when I get the marks back!

Chapter 6: Food

I couldn't speak about France without mentioning some of the yummy foods that I've tried so far. So here goes...

Camembert, I camembert believe how nice it is! Haha, ok I'll stop now! I've always loved camembert, it's really yummy, so I couldn't wait to eat it in France, with my baguette, thinking to myself: *Je suis française!*

Camembert is a type of soft cheese for those who weren't aware. It can be eaten simply with bread and butter or you can bake it so it goes all squishy in the middle and then you can dunk things in it.

Another interesting food I tried was sushi. I have always wanted to try sushi, just once, to see what it tastes like, so when I was invited out for lunch to a sushi bar, I was really looking forward to it! Interestingly, the French are obsessed with sushi. I was not expecting that.

We went to a place called Planet Sushi, and I remember thinking before, sushi isn't very big, I'll probably still be hungry afterwards. I was wrong. The portions were massive, I had this big plate of sushi, a big bowl of rice and a bowl of vegetables. I was stuffed! It filled me up so much that I didn't eat for the rest of the day.

But how was my first experience of eating sushi? It's actually quite nice, I wouldn't eat it all the time and I wouldn't think Oh let's go out for sushi! Because although it was nice it does seem a bit weird eating cold fish and rice, I think it'd taste nicer hot. Despite that, that's another thing ticked off the bucket list and a fun experience- you should've seen me trying to use the chopsticks!

Despite sushi seeming to be trendy, France are more traditionally well-known for their cakes and pastries, some of these include:

Croissants and pain au chocolat.
In some places these are called *'viennoise'* which is confusing because I ordered it expecting Viennese Whirls or something, not croissants and pain au chocolats.

Tarte aux Framboises (a raspberry tart)
I think this was one of the tastiest cakes I've ever eaten, the tartness of the raspberries with the sweetness of the filling was really yummy!!

Lemon meringue pie
This cake was lovely too! I think my favourite thing about France so far is the cakes! The best place for cakes here seems to be Brioche Dorée where you can get any hot drink and a patisserie cake for 3 euros 90! And when I went in yesterday (it was only my second time there) they gave me a loyalty card, so now I can collect points every time I eat cake! Clever.

A very warming dish is cassoulet, and it's perfect for the winter months. It looks a bit like sausages and beans, and I will admit it does taste a bit like sausages and beans, but it's not, it's cassoulet. If we're going to be precise about it, cassoulet is a rich, slow-cooked casserole from the South of France. It generally contains pork (hence the sausages) and white beans. Traditionally cassoulet gets its name from the dish it's cooked in: a casserole dish.

I was lucky to try authentic French crepes; cooked by my French friend Meggy. Crepes are exactly like pancakes, but not as thick. Just don't say that to a French person! According to my French friend Meggy, crepes are completely different from pancakes!

How to make crepes:

Use exactly the same ingredients as you would use for pancakes: flour, eggs and milk. Whisk the mixture well. Heat a pan with some oil in and when the pan is hot add a cup or ladle of mixture and then you're cooking crepes!

Here in France crepes are traditionally eaten with Nutella, (the French seem obsessed with Nutella! There were even fights in the supermarkets when Nutella was on offer!)

Interestingly there is a special way to eat crepes, they fold them up in a special way, a bit like if you fold a filter paper. In half, in half and in half again, to make a small triangle, like in the picture below. And the idea is that you eat from the wider end, because if you eat from the pointed end, you end up covered in chocolate.

Another yummy thing I tried was Galette de Rois is a pie traditionally eaten on the 6th January to celebrate the arrival of the 3 wise men.

It is a puff pastry pie filled with frangipane. Inside it also holds a *fève,* a small figurine. Whoever has the figurine in their piece is crowned King for the day and gets to wear the crown. It's very tasty!

Then we have le gratin 'blue mountain'. This was probably one of the yummiest French dishes I got to try when I was eating out and about. It was a potato gratin with gorgonzola (a blue cheese) and onions with some salad on the side. It was really tasty! I really like cheese, especially blue cheese so I think it was the perfect dish!

To follow my favourite main dish, here was my favourite French dessert. It's called 'Une religieuse'

What is it?

It's basically like two profiteroles stacked on top of each other...but it's different...

My religieuse in this picture was coffee flavoured, so each profiterole or choux pastry ball was filled with a coffee cream, and then coated with a coffee icing. Yum!

Why is it called a Religieuse?

This is what I really wanted to know, why is it called a religieuse?? That would mean religious in English, right? Do they eat it at church? Actually, religieuse in this case means nun. So, the cake is supposed to resemble a nun. And no, as far as I'm aware they don't eat it in church.

Is it nice?

Haha, silly question! It was delicious! I can't wait to eat another!

Is it easy to make?

Yes, surprisingly! I tried myself when I returned from my Year Abroad (I was missing them so much!) and considering it was my first time even making choux pastry, I was pretty chuffed with my results. It doesn't quite look the same, but it tasted great.

Chapter 7: Culture Shock

So, I spoke a bit about cultural differences and the shock of a new culture when I went to Spain, here's the French version including all the things I learnt during my first month in France.

Survival info: Milk

WARNING: Lait fermenté does not mean Pasteurised milk like I thought it did. In fact, Lait fermenté or fermented milk (yes, it actually exists), is more like the milk version of sour cream. It tastes like gone off milk and smells of stinky cheese. It is NOT normal milk. And yes, I didn't realise this until it was in my tea and I was drinking zed tea.

Normal milk in France is called: Lait frais (fresh milk) and the blue top means it's semi-skimmed. So to avoid dodgy tea, look carefully at the label.

Je ne peux pas esperer de te voir does not mean I can't wait to see you. To a French person this sounds more like, I can't wait not to see you, as in I don't want to see you. Which is the complete opposite of what you want to say. So, if you're trying to say I can't wait to see you it's better to say: J'ai hâte de te voir...as you can see I learnt this one the hard way!

How the washing machines work. Now I like to think that I'm a fairly chilled out person, but this was kind of stressful. Jeton. A new word. Jeter is the word to throw. Jeton means token. Big difference.

I learnt this new word the first time I used the washing machines in my halls of residence. I must've spent about 15 minutes thinking the sign was telling me to throw my washing in. And after attempting to insert a Euro into the coin slot, it still wouldn't fit. None of my coins would fit. Then my washing got stuck in the machine. I spent the next 5 minutes trying to get the door open again.

I took my unwashed washing back up to my room and thought about the word jeton. Looked it up on wordreference.... Jeton means token...

I had to go to reception to buy these tokens which I could insert into the machine, hence why my Euro wouldn't fit in it.

The reception desk was closed until the next afternoon.

Now I know about the jetons I've had no trouble using the washing machines, in fact I even ended up teaching other people how to use them.

Another big difference was how the buses work.

My first bus journey was cool. Completely unplanned. I got lost on the way home from Lidl, like really lost. I'd walked half an hour in the wrong direction. I knew around about where I was, and I knew that walking back would take me a good 45 mins providing I didn't get lost again, and my shopping was heavy, so I decided to get the bus. And it was fine! 15 minutes, I got off at the right stop, perfect! But here's the lowdown on important stuff you should know because as a foreigner it does seem a bit odd.

On the bus you either get a 1 journey or two journeys (like single or return) but I don't think it matters if you use your second journey that day or if you go another day, I've not tried that yet. They load it onto a reusable ticket which you then have to scan on the bus. If you don't scan your ticket you get a fine. So, make sure you scan your ticket. Then you're all set!

You can also buy 10 journey tickets or a student card, but they can't be bought on the bus, for those you have to go to the bus station in the centre of town.

Despite the reliability of the buses in Tours, creating a university timetable is...somewhat challenging.

You have to find each different module on their online system, each one is on a different screen, and from there you must build your timetable from scratch. There is no possible way to view your entire timetable together, you must first build it yourself on your own piece of paper or on a word document. So, if you want to double check the time or room of a class, you have to try and remember the series of buttons you originally clicked on to finally view that class. To sum it up, don't double check, you'll be there for about half an hour searching for it.

Moreover, walking halfway across town with a baguette in your hand here doesn't look weird. Off I went back home yesterday, la la la, with my baguette in hand, brandishing it a bit like a lightsaber, thinking oh I feel so French now! And thinking that it was probably just one of those stereotypes, all French people carry bread, and they all wear berets and stripy tops. The baguette thing is true, everyone had one! And berets, well I've seen a lot of men wearing berets or caps, so I'd say that one's true too. I haven't seen many stripy tops yet though, or people wearing garlic.

The baguette, the most typically French food there is, and one of the yummiest! The French stick, or baguette is an intrinsic part of French culture, to the point that Macron has announced that all French baguettes should be UNESCO listed treasures! It sounds a bit weird, but here the baguette is like our Roast Dinners or English Breakfasts, they are part of the culture and way of life here.

What is a baguette?

Obviously, a baguette is bread, (but a French person will probably tell you that it's so much more than just bread!) It's a tradition here to buy your bread daily from the boulangeries (bakeries), as unlike the bread we buy normally in England, baguettes don't contain any preservatives and are only made to last a day.

As a foreigner here in France I just assumed you could only buy one type of baguette, or maybe two, a white one and a wholemeal one. It was only upon my first visit to the boulangerie the other day that I realised I was wrong!

In your bog-standard bakery you can buy about 10 different types of French stick. When I visited one in Tours you could get an original French stick, a traditional one, a rustic one.... the list was endless!

Tips for visiting a boulangerie:

Work out what you want before you get in the queue. There is always a long queue in the boulangeries so if you know what you want you won't have to listen to a load of French people tut at you whilst you're trying to work it out at the till. Plus, by the time you're in the queue you'll get distracted by all the nice cakes they have, so if you haven't already decided you'll come away with a load of cakes instead of your bread, which isn't always a bad thing!

Another interesting difference is that it doesn't get light here until about 9am and then it's dark again by 5pm. I know that it's winter, but after 4 months in sunny Spain, I feel like I'm now living in eternal darkness! It's very cloudy here too, a lot like England. Despite this, wow, when the sky is blue, and the sun is out, it's very pretty!

I was also surprised to learn that I know more French than I gave myself credit for. This has been what has surprised me most. Problems with washing, making timetables, I was expecting all of that. I was also expecting to struggle understanding people, to be permanently saying: pouvez-vous repeter s'il vous plait? I think I've only said it 3/4 times so far, which I'm pretty chuffed about. I hadn't spoken properly in French since May, so I thought I'd forgotten it all, but I've actually remembered more than I thought! Yay!

French people at uni never sleep though. My timetable (for now at least) looks quite nice, I've only got one 8am start and I'm finished by 5 most days. However, my poor friend Meggy has some days where she starts at 8am and finishes at 7pm. And she only has two breaks, one for lunch and the other in the afternoon. Crazy! They don't even have a siesta here, how do they do it?

In addition to this, I am surprised quite how many people here smoke.

It's one of the stereotypes that is true. The shocking thing is that it's predominantly young people who smoke here, which means I see people smoking all the time because I'm at a French uni...

In a Tandem with a French student the other day I discovered that in France, smoking is not seen as disgusting, it is seen as classy and sophisticated. This surprised me a lot as in the UK we have a very negative view on smoking and not many youngsters smoke nowadays. My tandem partner only told me this after I'd mentioned how disgusting smoking was...luckily, he doesn't smoke!

In my opinion, the fact that French people smoke is part of the French hypocrisy, they are all obsessed with their figure, eating healthy and almost everyone here rides a bike, and yet despite this health complex they are all smoking themselves to an early death...

Conclusion: don't smoke!

If that wasn't enough, French people seem a wee bit more judgemental than us Brits. I mentioned it a little bit before, but it's very noticeable.

I have seen, and even some of my French friends agree with me, that the French judge more than us Brits. Every time I go by bus, or I go to the shops, or even when I'm at uni, people look at me, (and at other people) and they judge me by what I'm wearing.

I'd like to say that I've gotten used to the staring and that it doesn't bother me, but it's difficult. It is quite funny though...often when I was in France I would wear really bright coloured clothes with clashing colours just to wind them up and make them think: Oh my gosh! What is she wearing?

Interestingly, the French are still judgmental about your clothing when it's minus 4 degrees. Personally, when it's that cold, I don't care what I'm wearing or what I look like, I just want to be warm and comfy. So I really don't understand the mentality of people like this; if you want to freeze and die by wearing stupid clothes...be my guest.

Grumbling, however, is something that really makes me laugh! All French people seem to do it!

The other day I was in the queue in a shop and there was a woman in front of me in the queue. We'd been waiting about 5 minutes maybe when she started making these weird grumbling noises like: Huuuhhh! Grrrrr! Errrr! And I couldn't stop smiling!

She kept looking at me as if to say: "Are you not going to do the same? We've been waiting far too long you know!"

On the way back from this shopping trip, we discovered that the tram makes noises!
Ok, so this is a bit weird, there's this lady who sings like: da dah dah, when you're on the tram to help people not to fall asleep and miss their stop. But every time I hear the noise I'm thinking: 'Oh what's that? Who's singing?'

One point I must mention though, is the attitude of the French towards the English.

Now, of course, the French and us Brits haven't always gotten on, just look at our history. But I never paid it much notice. I don't hold a grudge against French people, so why would they hold one against me? However, often here in Tours, if I know I'll never see the person again, when they ask me where I'm from, I say I'm from Spain; not from England.

I am very proud of being British but every time I say I'm from England the person I'm speaking to says 'Oh'. I'm not sure what we've done, is it Brexit? Or just the life-long disputes between Great Britain and France? But the French don't seem to like me when they know I'm British...luckily, I know enough Spanish to believably be a Spaniard.

Despite these difficulties settling in: I've survived one month in France! I can't believe it!

I've done everything from telling people I'm preoccupied instead of worried, filled out enough forms to sink a battleship and been stared at like I'm an alien!

But I have had a good time so far, I've eaten lots of cakes, tried some French foods like cassoulet, ratatouille, the famous baguette and cheese. I've visited the castle (kind of) and a few places of interest and I finally seem to be settling in a bit more.

I think this month has been quite difficult because I arrived ready and excited to get going. Therefore, everything's felt quite slow and after having such an amazing time in Spain, it's been hard to adjust to French life because the French culture and Spanish cultures, despite having many similarities are also very, very different. It's been strange in that respect because I've missed Ronda, the weather, the people, my friends, the food and the tapas and the beautiful views so much.

Tours is different, the food here is nice as well, the weather is nice...if you like rain! But it's a lot harder to get to know people. However, I have now officially survived 1 month at university in France! After all the annoying forms and jumping through a million hoops, sitting in lessons where a French teacher 'corrected' my English, making it not make any sense and other lessons where you have to sit listen and write down practically every word the teacher says for 2 hours. I must say I'm pretty proud of myself. There have been many occasions where I've wanted to say, 'I've had enough,' and hop on the first flight back to Spain or England, but I have done it!

I think I've pretty much finished all the forms (though I won't say it too loud, because every time I think they're done, they seem to find another form!) and I'm now in classes that I enjoy more, with people who are nice and friendly (well most of them) and I think my French is improving, especially my listening, in week 1 my notes were very sparse, I just wrote what I could understand, but now they seem longer as I understand more. My Monday literature class involves sitting and listening to the teacher talk at us for two hours so I think when I can understand almost every word she says, (she speaks very softly- even with a microphone and very quickly) I'll know for sure I've improved!

So here's to the next few months, there are some exciting things coming up, wine tasting, a trip to the zoo, there's even a chocolate event going on in Tours! Oh and I have to study too; I have about a million books to read for my literature courses!

Chapter 8: The ESN trips

In Tours they have this association called the ESN, which stands for Erasmus Student Network. It is brilliant. It's basically a group for all of the Erasmus and International students at the University and it has made it a lot easier for me to get to know people and make friends.

Another great thing about the ESN is that they organise trips for us, so we can go out and explore the local area and learn more about the history and culture. The bonus is the trips are also subsidised, so they work out a lot cheaper than if you were to go on your own.

It's February at the moment, and so far, I've done two trips with them, one to the Vouvray wine caves and another to Beauval Zoo. Let me tell you about my adventures so far…

My first trip with the ESN was to the Vouvray wine caves. Vouvray is just West of Tours and is easily accessible from Tours by bus. Vouvray is famous for its white wines and its sparkling wines.

What did I do at the caves?

We had a guided tour of the wine caves and learnt all about how they store the wine and how the wine is produced. I thought that once it was in the bottle it stays there, but actually after the wine has matured it must be transferred to a new, clean bottle. So, it was interesting to know how they did that without the sparkling wine losing its bubbles.

Then we got the chance to taste 4 different wines. 2 were sparkling wines and the other two were white wines. They were all very tasty, especially the two sparkling wines and the dry white wine. I wasn't too keen on the sweet white wine. And we also got to eat some pastries, which were like mini-éclairs. Yum!

All in all it was a lovely day and I made some new friends as well!

Vouvray was where I first met Rebekka. Rebekka is German which is great because we always speak French together, as it's our common language. She studies law, so she's in a different building to me, but she's been in Tours since September, so she knows a lot more about the area and what there is to do.

I also got to know Sofie and Raiza a lot better too. Sofie is Swedish, I first met her in my translation class on my very first day. Raiza is Canadian. We have Children's literature and Italian together, so we should get to know each other a bit more.

I also met Zach, for the second time. The first time was in the launderette when I taught him how to use a washing machine, and now here he is again, with his baseball cap, looking so typically American. The first time I met him, I didn't realise we'd be friends, but talking to him again at the caves, I realised he's not just clueless, he's also very friendly and funny.

My second trip was a few weeks after, when I knew people a bit better, this was nice as I enjoyed myself a lot more. I spent most of the day with Sofie and Rebekka and we also saw Zach and Macey a bit too.

This trip was to Beauval Zoo. This zoo is actually said to be the best in France. Now I haven't visited any other zoos in France, but I must say this zoo was amazing, and certainly lives up to the claims and it's only an hour and a half away from Tours.

What did we do at the zoo?

Well, obviously we saw the animals and wow, we saw a lot of them! We saw lions, tigers, meerkats, rhinos, elephants, gorillas, jaguars and pandas, just to name but a few! And I learnt lots of new animal vocabulary in French!

It was a great day, yes it was cold, yes it was raining, but we still made the most of our day at the zoo. I really liked seeing the pandas because I'd never seen pandas in real life before, so that was quite special. There were two pandas, the mum and the baby who was born in august. The baby one was really cute.

I also enjoyed seeing the lions and tigers. I don't think I've ever seen lions and tigers so active before! They were running around, playing, enjoying themselves, it was magnificent to see these marvellous creatures in action!

We spent the whole day exploring the zoo, we saw a sea lion show which was very impressive, and we watched them feed the elephants, which was also really cool! It was funny watching the elephant's trunk suck up the food to put it in its mouth. I think we had just enough time to see everything, with a break for some lunch and a small break at the end before we hopped back on the bus.

If you get the chance to visit Beauval Zoo, you really should go! I would say it's perhaps the best zoo that I've ever visited. There's such a large variety of animals who are all well looked after, they all seem happy and they have lots of space to run around in.

Conclusion: the ESN trips are definitely worth it!

Chapter 9: Half term and travelling

The great thing about studying is that you get half term holidays, which provide the perfect opportunity to travel and make the most of being in another country. Luckily, France (when they're not striking) have very good transport and train services, so my friends and I decided we'd do a few daytrips to local towns, just to get an insight into what life is like in the smaller French towns and to visit a couple of the 200 castles situated in the Loire Valley.

On the Tuesday, Sofie and I went to Blois for the day. We went across on the train which in true French fashion arrived 10 minutes late. Off we went, hurtling towards Blois. Blois isn't too far away from Tours, it took us 40 minutes on the TGV and was only the 4th stop along.

It was a beautiful sunny day in Blois.

Sunny, yes.

Freezing cold, yes.

It got down to -9 at one point, so I was very pleased that I'd worn lots of layers! In the afternoon we were even greeted by some snow! It was so cold, the snow would land on my hand and take about 30 seconds to melt away, it was really cool to look at the snowflakes before they melted, because normally they melt far too quickly for me to see them.

When we arrived in Blois we made our way straight to the castle (in search of toilets, as most public toilets in France you have to pay for). The castle was really cool! The main characteristic of this castle is the pretty staircase that winds around the middle of the building. The castle was decked out as it would've been in the 1600's when it was home to the King of France, so it had very funky coloured wallpaper, referred to as 'gothic style'.

This castle may look small, but it is home to 564 rooms, of which over 100 are bedrooms, and there are 75 staircases. The first part of the castle was built in the 13th Century by the Count of Blois. Since then it was inhabited by several Kings including: Louis XII, Francois I, Henry III, Henry IV and finally Gaston d'Orleans (the brother of Louis XIII, who received it as a wedding gift). Each inhabitant made his mark on the castle, adding extra rooms and building new wings/ staircases.

In 1841 the castle was classified as a historical monument and it was restored. Then it was opened as a museum.

It was very interesting to look around the castle and we even found out that the castle was made from limestone, slate and brick, all local rocks that can be sourced and created nearby. I thought this was very interesting as it now makes sense why most of the buildings in and around Tours are white with grey roofs, the white is the local limestone and the grey is the slate.

After exploring the castle, we decided to have lunch and we found a cool "Japanese and Vietnamese" restaurant. I have never been to a Japanese and Vietnamese restaurant before, (I never knew such thing existed really), so it was a fun experience. I ate Miso Soup for the first time, which is actually really tasty, it's like a mushroom broth, with leek, mushroom and bits of soya floating in it, it was lovely and warming. Then I had beef with mushrooms and rice. Yum yum. I even tried a Thai beer called Singha Beer. And I think I'm getting a bit better at using chopsticks!

Then it was time to do some exploring! We braved the cold (and the snow that had begun to fall) and explored the town. We found a massive cathedral and the town hall, and as we descended down some of the smaller streets in Blois, with the old architecture and the snow falling, it felt as if we'd entered the world of Harry Potter!

We must've been somewhere between Hogsmead and Diagon Alley.

We sheltered in some shops for a bit whilst the snow stopped and then we had a look at the Loire River, the river looked a lot higher up in Blois than it had in Tours. On the rest of our travels we found a cute cat that I was going to take home and a weird art museum which looked quite funky from the outside.

As the day began to draw to a close we huddled in a church hoping it would be warm (no such luck) and saw a cool statue of Mary which everyone in the church prayed to. And then we found a nice, little café where we stayed to keep warm whilst we waited for the train back.

As our train hurtled back to Tours in the dark, it felt kind of spooky, and despite our excellent day in Blois, I couldn't wait to get back home and warm up again!

In the middle of my half term, dodging the snow, I took the plunge and went to the hairdressers. A visit to the hairdressers in France...what could go wrong?

I actually did it! Without any problems! I was scared, especially to start with when she asked me what I wanted. She must've listed about a million different things and I responded: just a haircut please.

The second thing is that in France you can't say: Can you cut of about an inch? Because inches don't exist here in

France, so you have to say: can you cut off two centimetres please? (which seems very precise!)

Also the lady didn't speak much, I don't know if it's normal, because I know in England my hairdresser talks a lot! We spend ages chatting away. And well when I'm nervous I talk a lot too. I talk nineteen to a dozen anyway, but I talk even more if I'm nervous. So, there I was sat there in the hairdressers speaking nonsense (in French) about the weather, my studies and by the end we'd actually managed to have a conversation, (I got the vibe she couldn't chat and cut hair at the same time).

So, to sum it up, I'd say that going to the hairdressers in another country is a good idea for learning new hairdresser related vocab and for practising the language. However, I must admit, I wouldn't have gone to the hairdressers if I hadn't have really needed to go.

On the Friday of my half term, when the snow had finally melted, it was time for another daytrip, and this time I went with Zach and Alina and our port of call was Amboise.

Amboise is located just West of Tours. It was the second stop on the train, just after Saint Pierre de Corps, it only took about 20 minutes to get there. It was a very pretty and friendly place.

We also, *surprise surprise* visited the castle! The castle in Amboise was very interesting. The Italian painter Leonardo da Vinci spent most of his adult life in Amboise and his grave is actually inside the chapel at the castle.

Then we went for a walk past Leonardo da Vinci's previous home Clos Luce, the gardens there looked very pretty! And then we popped into a small boulangerie cafe for a coffee and a cake to warm ourselves up again before we headed back to Tours!

Our return to Tours marked a very special and important moment during my stay: it was the moment I ate my first macaron in Tours!

I know what you're thinking: Abi, the lover of food didn't eat her first macaron in tours until she'd been there for 2 months! I know, I know, I can't believe it either! But the important thing is that now I have eaten my first macaron! And I've eaten macarons before, just not in Tours!

So, it was on the way back from Amboise, we'd just arrived back in Tours train station. We were just heading out, when we saw a macaron shop. Literally it only sold macarons! They had practically every single colour imaginable! The place was called: *Le Monde de Macarons* too! (The world of Macarons!) And they were cheaper there than in other places, so I had to try one! I tried the blueberry one, it was really nice! Zach tried a vanilla one, which he enjoyed too.

Chapter 10: The Students Strike!

About a week after the holidays, the drama began. The students went on strike. This was something I hadn't even consider when I first arrived and knowing I had to pass all of my subjects with at least 10/20 worried me.

There'd been some banners and signs up in Tanneurs (my university building) for a few weeks, but I hadn't thought much of it, France is renowned for striking.

The posters are about this new law that Macron wants to impose regarding access to university. This law is going to change who can get into university. At the moment in France anybody can go to university and do any course, regardless of their grades. These new changes will mean that students need to have certain grades to access certain courses, which makes sense, especially for things like medicine.

Personally, I think this makes sense, what's the point in doing a course which you don't understand because you don't have the right knowledge? Also, these new changes could mean that the courses are more focussed on the subject because there won't be as many people on the course who aren't interested in it. During my time here so far, I have noticed that a lot of people only go to university because it's free and easy to get into. Although a free, open system can be good, a lot of people go not intending to work hard and not interested in getting a good degree.

However, obviously, a lot of students don't agree with this new law, so they've gone on strike to show the world how they feel about these changes. This meant that when I arrived at uni at 8am on Thursday morning for my class, I couldn't get into the building...the students had barricaded all of the doors and formed a picket line...

On one hand I was happy- no classes today yay! On the other hand, I'd gotten up at 6:30 for nothing! So I decided that the least I deserved was a second breakfast! I chose chouquettes, they're small balls of choux pastry dipped in sugar, yummy!

After my chouquettes I met my tandem and her friend in a café in Place Plume, we spoke for 4 hours (just in French!) I don't think I've ever spoken in French for that long! It was great practise! Then I went back home for lunch...but I got lost finding the bus stop and ended up finding a Basilica; it's amazing what you find here when you're lost! So, I explored a bit and then went home, an exciting day!

After that day I thought, 'Ah well, that's it, they've made their point, strikes over'... not quite...

In fact, the strikes lasted about 5 weeks in the end. To my surprise, all of the blockades and moving of classes was nothing in comparison to what was happening at other universities, some of my friends told me their whole campus was on lockdown by the police and others mentioned that their French friends had been attacked with tear gas when trying to get to their exams.

Below you have some more information on the strikes at Tours. It was getting very frustrating...here's what I wrote at the time of the strikes.

Top 3 things I hate about the student strikes at Tours:

1. They always strike on a Thursday here and it's only at Tanneurs

Yes, that's right, they decide to strike on the day that I have four different classes. Every single other day I only have one or two classes. And if I wasn't a languages student at Tanneurs my lessons would still be on, as it's only the languages/humanities and social sciences building, Tanneurs, which is closed.

2. Macron isn't going to listen to a group of students striking at Tours, so in reality, they are striking for no reason

I'm sorry, but if I was the President of France I probably wouldn't even be aware that students at Tours were on strike, let alone that they were on strike because of one of my new laws. So really, is there a point in striking?

3. No lessons = bored Abi

After a week of many cancellations (practically every one of my lessons has been cancelled) I was delighted that Thursday would be my first 'proper' day back at uni...until

Wednesday evening when I got an email about the strikes. The only good thing was that this time I received an email, so I didn't have to get up at 6:30 for no reason.

But is EVERYTHING cancelled when they have a strike?
Not quite everything. My Translation Class is just for exchange students, so the teacher emailed us all and planned to do the lesson in another building, so we didn't miss out on the lesson which I thought was lovely of her. And then in the evening there was a poetry event on at Tanneurs which also still took place.

Why do they cancel all of the lessons?
Lessons here are 'compulsory', if you are not present you are supposed to provide a doctor's note, e.g., you can only not go to class if you're sick or dying. Therefore, if certain students decide to strike the uni says that absences won't be penalised, because here in France its part of their rights to be allowed to strike (interesting right). This surprised me as I've never before seen students striking, it's normally the teachers in the UK, and if students strike it's not normally taken as seriously and it's your fault if you miss out on a lesson.

So what do you do when there are strikes?
Well I wasn't stood at the picket line I can tell you that! Haha, I still had one of my lessons luckily, and then I bought a cool newspaper called Le Canard Enchaîné, I think it's a bit satirical, I'll let you know when I've gotten around to reading it! And then in the afternoon Rebekka and I went up to Tanneurs for the poetry event. The poetry event, unfortunately, was really boring, so we left

after half an hour and had a walk around the river, making the most of the sunshine!

Funny thing was that after the student strikes, the trains decided to strike as well, for 2 days a week from April to July...

I can honestly say I truly experienced French culture!

Chapter 11: February

February was cold in France. We had snow for most of the month which made things interesting.

One Tuesday after class, Sofie, Erik, Meggy and I decided to go to Ikea. Ikea, as I predicted is pretty much the same in every country, but this was a unique experience: going around Ikea with two Swedish people (and a French person).

Ikea is a Swedish company, and as you all probably know, the names for all of the items sold in Ikea make no sense. This is because they're in Swedish, a lamp is a lamp...oh and that one's a blue lamp...that's a big lamp. It means stuff to them. And as for the food section, well I've never seen anyone get so excited over frozen meatballs! I don't normally even look at the food bit, and here were Sofie and Erik: Oh, that's my jam from home! My bread! Oh I missed this so much!

I can honestly say you haven't been to Ikea, until you've been with Swedish people.

After our trip to Ikea, Sofie and Erik decided to stay to eat some meatballs for dinner, whilst Meggy and I went to Carrefour to get ingredients to make Crepes.

So we hopped on the bus to Meggy's house and made our crepes and afterwards we had a natter...the next time I looked at the clock it was 10 at night...and it was still snowing.

Knowing I had a class at 8:30 the next day, I went to go and wait at the bus stop to get home. We waited half an hour, until a guy informed us that the buses had been stopped for the snow. So, there I was, stranded in the dodgy part of town, in the heavy snow, at night.

Luckily, Meggy let me stay with her. I could've walked 40 minutes back home, but I didn't know the area well and it wasn't a nice area to be walking late at night, so it didn't seem like a great idea.

So instead, we made a snowman! At 11 at night, why not?

I think I only slept about four hours that night. I woke up at 6:30 and got the bus home so I could shower and change my clothes before my class at 8:30. Despite the snow and everything, I managed to get to class on time, unlike our teacher! It was an adventure, but not one that I'll be repeating any time soon! When it snows again, I'll be staying in I think.

The snow finally let off in the last week of February, so Rebekka and I went to the film festival.

We saw a Spanish film. Yes, that's right, I went to watch a Spanish film, in France with my German friend, not confusing at all! It was the first time I've watched a Spanish film with French subtitles, so that was interesting, when I didn't know the Spanish word I looked at the French subtitles and thought, nope haven't got a clue what that word is either! The most difficult bit was afterwards, after 2 hours listening to Spanish, to speak French with my German friend...I spent the whole time translating from

Spanish in my head, so it sounded a bit weird, but good practise!

The film was called: "La danza de la realidad," (La danse de réalité in French and The dance of reality in English). It's an interesting film. It's very weird (like all Spanish films) but also very political. It's set in Chile and there are references to several different dictatorships, and shows the struggle of a man who at first wanted to kill the dictator and then came to identify with the dictator, who is then captured and then the dictatorship is ended, and I think another dictator was in charge? There were a lot of dictators, even the Nazis were involved at some point, so I got a bit confused. It was hard to interpret because the main character owned a circus, his wife sang every word and everyone in the town was dressed as circus characters. I understood all the words they were saying (even the wife who sang every word) but there was a deeper, historical meaning to everything that was completely lost on me. It left me thinking, what?

But it was kind of funny in a, "What have I just watched" sort of way and I learnt a lot about French cinema culture. They all clapped at the end of the film and they all stayed behind afterwards to debate about the film- not something we do in the UK! And because it was a special event it was free entry...free entry, we never have that in the UK!

At this point I'm really settling in to life in France and I'm learning to understand and appreciate their culture. The one thing I love the most about French culture is the French people's love for food. I am a big foodie and love trying new foods, so it's great to be here in France and try lot of new things. For me, the French people's love of food is evident here, almost every restaurant or café has at least one type of sign mentioning the word "gourmand" which would translate as food lover or foodie in English. And the fact that every corner houses a small boulangerie full of bread and more pastries and cakes than you can poke a finger at! Everyone walks down the road brandishing their baguettes (it's seen as completely normal here) and most people who work here seem to have a 2-hour break for their lunch.

Bonne dégustation!

Chapter 12: Macron and March

I've often thought that language learning is in stages. This afternoon after my lesson I popped into the supermarket just to pick up a couple bits and they had changed their loyalty cards. So, after I'd got my shopping I had to go to a desk to get my card changed over so all of my current points would go onto the new card. The lady could tell I was foreign. And when I told her my date of birth, doing all the numbers for the year, she was amazed and said how good my French was. When you learn a language, things like that make you feel happy.

But anyway, stages of learning a language. I think you have the first stage when you first start learning and you're trying to get your head around grammar and vocabulary. Then you just wake up one day and everything clicks. From then on you have the second stage, the "I kind of know what I'm doing but I've still got a lot more to learn" phase. I feel that, from my experience, towards the end of this stage you seem to plateau a bit, it feels like you're not learning as much anymore and it can be hard to stay motivated.

And that's when the third stage begins.

Suddenly when you speak to people it seems harder, they speak faster, they use words you may not recognise, this is the third stage. People know your level is good, they know you can understand so they speak to you how they'd normally speak with a native speaker. Obviously, I am at different levels in my languages, for Spanish, I'd say this

3rd stage began for me the moment I arrived in Ronda on my Year Abroad. However here in France, I'd say that moment is now. This week I have spoken with lots of different people and had to sort out lots of different things. At some points this week it feels like French has been getting harder, or my French is getting worse, but actually, the fact I'm finding it harder shows I'm learning more and I'm improving. And even just a small compliment from someone in a supermarket about your French can make you feel like you're almost getting there. Time to keep on learning!

As well as noticing changes to my linguistic abilities March was a month of travels…and studying, well when they weren't striking!

One Saturday, I went on a trip with the ESN to Chateau Chambord. This castle is the biggest and most magnificent (from the outside) in the Loire Valley, so it was a must-see!

Chambord is close to Blois, but it's difficult to get to unless you have a car (or you go on an organised trip like we did). We spent the afternoon exploring the castle and gardens, it was beautiful!

Then we visited a biscuit maker and got to sample different biscuits, all washed down with a glass of wine. The biscuits were tasty too, my favourites were the orange ones.

All in all, it was a lovely day with good company, good biscuits and good weather (18 degrees Celsius!!)

The next day I decided to learn a bit about the local history, most notably, the battle of Tours.

The battle of Tours took place in 732 between the French and the Arabs. The French forces were led by Charles Martel and the Arab forces by the General of the Al-Andalus army.

What I find most interesting about this battle is that Al-Andalus is in the South of Spain, now known as Andalusia, where I was last term. However, during this era, it was ruled by the Arabs, hence the large number of Arab words and sounds in the Spanish language and I must admit whilst I was there I saw many signs that said Al-Andalus which referred back to this part of their history.

The battle took place between Poitiers and Tours and at the end the French won, killing the Arab General and allowing the French to retake control of the South of France. The Arabic army retreated back to Spain.

Some people see Charles Martel as the saviour of Christianity, as this battle is seen as the start of one of the most important eras in the history of the world, showing the power of the French and hinting at the battles that were yet to come.

But hands down, one of my favourite March memories, asides from Macron visiting Tours; that was interesting. Everyone flocked to see him, it was like the Queen or a really important celebrity had arrived. I could never imagine the British public acting that way about any politician.

But asides from that, my favourite has to be my visit to the chocolate festival. They like their festivals in Europe, don't they?

I'd first seen this advertised back in January, so I'd been looking forward to it. A festival completely devoted to chocolate? Wow, it sounded like my kind of place! *Le salon de chocolat*, as it's called in French, was full of chocolate, with many exhibitors, all of whom are chocolate shops in Tours, I never realised there were so many!

First, we saw a display for an Easter egg decorating competition (I've just made it sound like it's for 5-year olds, they were professional chocolatiers!) And then we explored the fayre and tried lots of different chocolate!

The only chocolate I tried that I didn't like was a dark chocolate which was 100% cocoa. I didn't know 100% cocoa was even possible! It was very bitter. I normally like dark chocolate because you have the bitterness and the sweetness, but with the 100% cocoa there is no sweetness.

Another thing that surprised me is that they had a stall selling "Ice Rolls" it's like chocolate which is frozen, and they add fruit and then they roll it. It looked really cool!

My favourite chocolate of the day was the dark, minty chocolate, yum yum!

Chapter 13: Spring!

Tartiflette, mmm, potatoes, onion, bacon and cheese, what a great mixture! I'm talking about food again, aren't I?

Seriously though, if you were here, you'd completely understand. Until Friday I'd never actually tried Tartiflette on its own. I'd tried in in a roll and in a crepe, but not on its own, so I decided to have it for dinner! It was delicious! I would definitely recommend it!

In other food news this week...

I finally managed to find bacon! It's not the same as British bacon, I'd say the bacon here is more like streaky bacon, but it's bacon, which means I can have a bacon sandwich! Yay!

I also managed to find some 'Genoise Chocolat noir et Orange' aka Jaffa Cakes! Yum!

On the 21st March there was a Spring party in the town hall. It was great fun! First and foremost, we got to see inside the town hall which is amazing. It felt really cool, especially knowing that Macron had been in the same place just the week before! There was music, free champagne and nibbles and I even had my caricature drawn! What more could you want?

Then the following weekend, I decided to visit Orléans. Orléans, despite being smaller than Tours, it is the capital of the region Centre-Val de La Loire.

I was a bit nervous about the trip, it was the first time (asides from my arrival in Tours) that I would be travelling alone to somewhere completely unknown, and also the first time (and the last!) that I'd use the FlixBus service. So, I got up bright and breezy at 6:30 for my big adventure!

I had to take two different buses just to get to the Flixbus bus stop, which was fine, public transport (as long as there are no strikes) is very good and reliable, and so I made sure to arrive nice and early. The bus was due to leave Tours at 8:20 and everyone was on the bus, we were about to go, when:

BAM! disaster struck.

This dodgy looking guy started having a fit, it was obvious he'd taken drugs... 20 minutes later, the *pompiers* (yes, that's right, the firemen. I'm told the fireman deal with sick people here!) were there and after a while they managed to extract him from the bus and take him away.

Finally, 30 minutes later than expected we left. And eventually, after a stop for petrol and a long diversion, I made it to Orléans.

What is there to do in Orléans?

The most important thing you should do is see the Statue of Joan of Arc (Jeanne d'Arc). Set in the centre of the square it is very imposing and really pretty when the weather is nice, like it was for me! But who is Joan of Arc, and why is she so important?

I found the visit to Orléans very interesting because we have done quite a bit about her in class recently as she seems a very important figure to this region of France. However, it is a bit awkward because, very unfairly in my opinion, the French still blame us for burning her at the stake. It's not like I was even alive then! (I think they just use it as another excuse to hate us English people!)

There's a cathedral, that was massive. And the Loire River. Now this river, it's very long, has been in pretty much every city I've visited, Tours, Blois, Amboise and Orléans, but it's still worth a visit. Yes, it looks practically identical in all of the places, but I enjoy going to see it. In Orléans I sat on a bench and ate my baguette by the river. It's a nice place to sit and relax and soak up the sun!

Another thing I discovered in Orléans is the BD (bande dessiné, the comic books). Comic books are different here in France. In the UK it's mainly just children under 10 who read them, here everybody reads them! In celebration of this tradition I decided to buy myself one! I've finally finished reading all of the books for my French literature classes, so I can start reading the things that I want to read! It just so happens that what I want to read is a comic for children! I got one from the Asterix series: Asterix et Cléopatre (Asterix and Cleopatra).

I sat and started reading a bit of it on my train journey home. Yes, that's right, train home. After the morning's interesting events and the fact that the bus took twice as long, was an hour walk from the centre of town and wouldn't leave until 18:30, (if it ever arrived!) I decided it would be best (and safer) to get the train home.

Chapter 14: Making Memories

A Year Abroad is all about making memories, having great things to think back on. Things that make you think: Wow, I actually did that? Or things that surprise you and come unexpected. From my experience, my best memories of being away were the times spent with friends, be it just a casual meet up for a meal or drinks or going travelling somewhere.

One great memory was Easter Sunday. I decided to invite Rebekka, Sofie and Zach over for Easter lunch. This wasn't a traditional Easter lunch, as I didn't have an oven to cook a Roast and to make our multicultural meal complete, we all bought part of the meal. Zach was on drinks...after his recent pancake disaster, it was probably for the best! Rebekka was on starter and made a Spanish omelette, I was on main and cooked Chicken Curry with rice and Sofie made peanut buttercups for dessert.

The whole meal was delicious, and the only time I've had to say to people, please bring your own plate and cutlery, and if you want a chair, bring that too! Haha, it was fun, all bunched up in my tiny room eating and it was lovely to spend the afternoon with them.

In the evening Zach, Sofie and I went out for a drink. I could not believe how many people were out and about, on Easter Sunday! Normally, I spend the afternoon/evening of Easter Sunday at home with family, sometimes even the whole day, so to see some many

French people out and about was unexpected, but it made for a good atmosphere.

Another great day was the trip to La Rochelle with the ESN. The weather had been getting a lot nicer now, anywhere from 18 to 25 degrees, which was lovely!

We met at the train station at 7:45 which was a very early start, but it was worth it! It took us three hours to get to La Rochelle on the coach, so we arrived about 11 ish.

After getting lost because the driver dropped us off miles from the centre of town we finally found the Tourist Information desk where we met our guide for the guided tour. It was a bit dull and showery to begin with, but the guided tour was great. The lady was very interesting and informative, and I know my French has improved from being here as I managed to understand pretty much everything she told us. She explained a lot about the history of the town as a fishing port and a harbour and gave us lots of useful information on fun things to do in La Rochelle.

April, the month we went, is the peak season for mussels in La Rochelle and La Rochelle produces 50% of French shellfish (pretty cool) so we had to go and try some. Rebekka, Zach, Erik, Jeremie, Laura and I went to a seafood restaurant for lunch. Laura had plaice, Rebekka had fish and chips and the guys had shrimps with rice while I tried moule frites for the first time!

What are moule frites?

Moules are mussels, they are a type of shellfish. When you eat them you only eat the small, yellow oval inside, you don't eat the shell. And if the shell hasn't opened during cooking, the mussel isn't safe to eat, so don't try to prise the shell open if it's not already opened. I've tried mussels a couple times before, but it's only ever been one or two more Spanish style mussels with a paella, never a whole bowl full.

French style mussels are very different. They are cooked in a white wine sauce with garlic and onions, and each mussel is stuffed with herbs. They were amazing! And to make it even better they were served with a bowl of chips, (that's the *frites* part of the Moule Frites) Yum yum!

After lunch we headed to an ice cream shop for some ice cream because now the weather had warmed up, it was beautiful sunshine and 20 degrees, perfect ice cream weather! I had raspberry ice cream which was lovely.

Then we went and visited one of the towers. You can get a ticket which allows entry to all three towers for 7 euros, or for free if you're a student, so we all got in for free. The view of the town from the tower was beautiful!

Then we decided to go on a boat trip across the harbour, as it only costs 2 euros per journey and was a fantastic way to experience the harbour of La Rochelle. I remember as we turned the corner and were faced with a sea of a thousand boats all moored up, it was very impressive, and with the warm sun and blue skies it was wonderful!

Then we walked from there to the aquarium. The aquarium was fun, and we played: who can find what they just had for lunch. They had some really cool fishes and at the end there was a rainforest bit which was fun to explore.

We made a quick stop for a panini before hopping back on the coach to Tours again. I got home at 23:30 and I was shattered, a long day but a great day! If you ever get the chance to go to La Rochelle, you should definitely go. In my opinion, it would be a lovely place to visit or live because you have a mixture of the town and the countryside as the whole town is surrounded by fields and you also have the sea on your doorstep. The town also has a lot of character in comparison to other places in France. In La Rochelle you say goodbye to the Gothic and Renaissance style architecture and say hello to funky coloured houses and buildings.

On Sunday there was a picnic by the lake near Fac 2 Lions. Tired from my La Rochelle adventure the day before this was a lovely relaxed way to see everyone before the end of term. Everyone bought food, I bought blue cheese and crackers. And so, we sat and ate by the lake, the sun shining down on us. Then two hours later the Spaniards arrived, haha, bringing music and beer. It was a lovely afternoon but scary knowing that we only have a few more weeks left!

A few weeks later we had the exams. Uh-oh! In France, everything is marked out of 20, and I needed to get at least 10/20. For most subjects I wasn't too worried, I'd already done some of the assessments. But for a couple of my courses: Italian and Analyse d'oeuvres, there was only 1 exam, which was 100% of the mark, and I had no idea what to expect, particularly considering I'd missed over half of the Italian classes due to cancellations for strikes…

(You'll be pleased to know that I did pass in the end!)

The afternoon after my translation exam, I decided to stick around for a bit and ended up going to the supermarket with my Swedish friends Sofie and Erik. They had to make something from their country to take to their French class in the afternoon, so they were making the traditional Chocolate balls. (Chokladboll in Swedish).

So off we went to get the ingredients in Carrefour and then we had lunch in the uni canteen. After a yummy lunch of Steak, pasta and veg (a strange combination I know!) with chocolate tart for pudding, it was time to make the chocolate balls! And I got to help!

I'm not 100% sure of the exact quantities though I now know how to say sugar and cocoa powder in Swedish, but here were the ingredients:

Sugar
Butter
Oats
Cocoa powder
A couple teaspoons of coffee (coffee and water mixed together)
Vanilla extract
And shredded coconut to coat the balls

Basically we mixed all of the ingredients, starting with the butter and sugar, adding and mixing each ingredient separately. Then you shape them into balls and coat them in coconut.

They are very tasty! I'll definitely be making them again! :)

Chapter 15: A visit from home

I had been looking forward to this for weeks! Yes, I was enjoying myself in France, I had great friends and I was doing lots of fun and exciting things, but I couldn't wait to see my family. Asides from 2 weeks at Christmas, I hadn't seen them properly since September.

The question was; what were we going to do for the weekend?

My family arrived on the Thursday evening, exhausted for their day of travel. They were staying in a hotel just around the corner from me, which was great as I didn't have far to go to meet them. The Thursday evening, I just took them out for dinner and I showed them some cool places on the walk there and back.

On the Friday we went and did some proper exploring! After some brekkie at the boulangerie we headed off to the botanic garden, my favourite place in Tours. We did this massive walk, around the gardens, and then from there up to the Place du Monstre and Place Plume, across the bridge by the Loire and onto one of the islands. And then at 2pm, I had to go off for my French speaking class. My family seemed glad I was off to a lesson, relieved at the chance to have a rest after our exploration.

On the Saturday we went to the cathedral, the shops, the town hall and the law courts. And on Sunday morning we headed off on the tram to Fac 2 Lions to walk around the lake. In the afternoon, there was a carnival going on in the town centre. This year the theme was Around the World. It was the first time I'd been to a carnival, so I was very excited, and it was great to be there with my family too.

At the head of the carnival was a spinning globe and behind it were many different groups of people dressed up and dancing, representing many different countries. You had everything from a bagpipe band, steel drum players,

an American line dancing group, Brazilian carnival dancers and a Minions float. It was a lovely event and it was probably the first time I've seen the community of Tours come together like that, everyone dancing and enjoying themselves.

My family left on the Monday morning and I was sad to see them go. I'd had a lovely weekend with them and it'd made me realise how much I missed them, particularly my Mum!

Chapter 16: Getting out of your comfort zone

A Year Abroad is all about trying new things, getting out of your comfort zone and trying something new.

Back in March I entered a competition run by the University of Tours. You had to create a picture, poem, video or song about Tours explaining why you like Tours. As my filming and artistic abilities are limited, I decided to write a poem. Here is my poem:

Moi et mon sac à dos

Abigail Nobes

Mon sac à dos
Il est beau.
Mon sac à dos
Est espagnol.
Mais maintenant
On va partout
Moi et mon
Sac à dos

Voici les arbres
Et la fontaine
Où sommes-nous ?
Le jardin botanique

Et maintenant
Près de la Loire,
Nous avons une classe
Au Tanneurs

La classe est finie
Donc on y va
Voici le château
Et la cathédral

Des peintures partout
De la renaissance
À l'art moderne
« Nous sommes heureux »

Et pour un moment
On s'arrête
Une petite pause
Pour gringoter

Voici le Tramway
Juste à temps
On y va

Place du Monstre
Ensuite Place Plume
Des édifices stupéfiants
Moi et mon
Sac à dos

Voici les gens
Au marché des Halles,
La nourriture
Miam miam

Il fait beau
Aujourd'hui
Peut-être allons-nous
Au nord de Tours
Pour boire du Vouvray
Ou faire une balade
Moi et mon
Sac à dos

Il y a plein de choses à faire à Tours
Mais pars où
Devrait-on
Commencer ?
Moi et mon
Sac à dos

It's about my backpack and in the poem, I travel around Tours with my backpack and talk about different places.

At the end of April, they announced the winners of the competition, and much to my surprise, I was one of the four winners.

It was daunting as they made me read out my poem in French to everyone at the event and I got interviewed by a journalist, but I'm guessing my French must be improving! My advice: if you get the chance to enter competitions like this or do something completely different and random- go for it!

A few weeks after that surprising news, I was off on another ESN trip...

Visit the gardens and castle of Villandry they said. It'll be pretty they said. Go by bike they said. It's only 17km each way, they said... It'll be easy I thought! Haha :)

It was fine, I didn't die!

But the 29-degree sunny weather didn't exactly make it any easier.

It takes 1hr and a half to cycle to Villandry and it's a lovely bike ride through the countryside. One thing I noticed on my bike ride is that it's a lot nicer (and safer) riding a bike in France, than riding a bike in the UK. Firstly, it's more common to ride a bike in France so motorists are more accustomed to it, so they seem to have more respect for cyclists. Also, they seem to have more cycle lanes in France. The only issue, having to ride on the right...I figured that one out after I saw the cars driving towards me! Arggg!!

That was hilarious because all of my friends were following me thinking, Abi knows what she's doing. Forgetting that Abi is from Great Britain, where they drive on the left.

Long story cut short, we moved to the other side of the road...very quickly.

At long last we arrived at the castle! And all we wanted to do was sit down and relax, but as they say, no rest for the wicked and we were whizzed off on a guided tour of the chateau and gardens. The gardens in particular were stunning.

The gardens comprise of 7 hectares, with only 10 gardeners taking on this mammoth task, I was amazed. And the gardens even include a sun garden, featuring yellows, golds and oranges and a sky garden full of blues and pastel colours. After our tour we had 40 minutes to enjoy the garden, grab an ice cream (mine was raspberry and blackcurrant!) before we cycled back to Tours again. A tiring but fun day!

Conclusion of Part 2

On one of my last few days, all the exams done, the sun shining, we all met up for drinks. This was a lovely way to say goodbye to everyone. I'd met so many different people, from so many different corners of the globe. There was Sofie, Zach, Rebekka, Meggy, Jack and Macey; the people I'd speak most time with. And everyone else; the Chinese girls in my class who'd almost made me choke with laughter when they suggested eating cats, dogs and donkeys. The Canadians who were always so lovely to everyone; the Spaniards who always turned up late and the Italians who always dressed immaculately. But most importantly, the French people who helped me improve my French and made me feel welcome in their country, in particular, Camille, Emmanuelle and Meggy.

My Year Abroad has flown by. I knew it would go quickly, but I hadn't quite envisaged it would be over quite so soon.

Tours was such a different experience to Ronda. It was the first time I'd lived in a big city and I met so many people from so many different countries.

Studying was different to working, and I feel I certainly made the right decision. My French wasn't as good as my Spanish so having the support of being in a uni and the freedom to pick the courses I wanted made it a lot easier to improve my level. From the courses I picked I think I learnt a lot, possibly even more than I'd learnt in Spain, and having extra resources like the university library, so I could read French books and the tandem sessions, so I could speak to French people more really helped me gain confidence and make the most of being in Tours.

I will miss Tours, more so the people than the place itself, who made my time in Tours great.

So now you've heard about my adventures, it's time for you to go out there and have your own!

Part 3: Returning home

Going back home. That's the easy bit, right? You've spent a whole year away from home and you're excited to go back and see your family and friends again. But you're also leaving everything behind; the life you've created, the friends you've made, and it's difficult. If I had to describe it in just one word, I'd say it's bittersweet. You have the anticipation of heading home, resuming your British life again, seeing all your friends and family again but also the sadness of leaving the place you've only just gotten used to.

It's almost like having reverse culture shock. Culture shock to your own culture. I never knew it was possible until I experienced it myself. I was chatting to a friend the other day and she completely agreed with me, the hardest part of the Year Abroad is returning home.

When we were chatting we both mentioned how much we missed French baguettes; they're just not quite the same at home, and other things like the freedom to go out whenever and wherever you want and most importantly the people. Heading home is hard when all of your friends are either in full-time employment, or still studying, getting through those last exams and their dissertations, looking forward to graduation, and you know you've still got a whole year left of studying.

Not only this, but you will notice that over your Year Abroad you will change and grow, becoming a very different person than you were before. I noticed I'd become more independent, more confident and a lot more flexible and adaptable to new situations. It's worth remembering that you're not the only one who changes; everyone else in your life changes too. Whilst I was away a friend of mine had a baby, people got new jobs, my brother grew up a lot and everything feels different. I almost thought that everyone else's lives would be on pause while I was away, I'd come back and everything would be the same...another example of me being wrong!

Another challenge is getting used to speaking English 24/7 again. To start with it's exhausting, rather like speaking a foreign language when you first go abroad. Also, I keep forgetting English words. Either that or there'll be a Spanish or French word that means something I want to say, but doesn't exist in English, and I'll be thinking, "Do we have a word for that in English?"

In addition to this culture shock, I found I had homesickness in reverse. I noticed this mainly when I went from Spain to France. I missed Ronda, the people there, my job and the life I'd created for myself. I still miss it now sometimes. Though I'm sure that after the summer, when I'm back at uni again, I'll get so wrapped up in everything I won't have as much time to miss it as much.

The most important thing though: you did it, you survived a Year Abroad and you've really improved your language skills.

What does this mean though?

Well, it makes you a lot more employable for starters. You have the language skills, but also a lot of other transferable skills and experience. You've worked or studied abroad, you know how to be independent, how to cope in unusual situations and solve problems a lot better, and most importantly, you've learnt how to communicate with other people from other cultures.

So, now you're all done, the world is your oyster, so what are you waiting for? ☐

The FAQ section:

This FAQ section is split into various sections regarding different topics. These include:

- 5 things you should take on your Year Abroad
- Packing your case
- Travelling as a student: discount cards, tips and advice
- Budgeting
- The Erasmus forms
- Assessments: grading systems in foreign countries in comparison with the UK
- Assessments from your home university: examples from my uni
- How to cope with culture shock
- Keeping a record of your Year Abroad
- Working in Spain
- Studying Abroad
- Accommodation

If you have any questions regarding the year Abroad then hopefully you will find the answers in this section.

5 things you should take on your Year Abroad with you

Obviously, there are many things that you should take with you on your Year Abroad, but here are 5 things that I never thought I'd use/need but have found very useful and would be lost without them.

1. A sharpie

For me, this is incredibly useful for writing on my milk, ham or bread the date it was opened. Therefore, I know when it was opened and when I really shouldn't be eating/drinking it anymore.

If you are sharing your accommodation with other people, a Sharpie is very good for labelling your food so somebody else doesn't eat it.

2. A mini travel sewing kit

Never thought I'd actually use it, but it's come in handy. I had to sew up my bag and sew a button onto something. You never know when you might need a needle and thread, so it's always best to have it just in case!

3. Spare pair of glasses

I mentioned this before when speaking about my time in Spain. If you're a glasses wearer then this is a must! You never know when you might have an issue with your glasses so just in case it's good to have a spare pair. Especially if you're like me and you're completely blind without your glasses!!

4. Scissors

But why? Well, if your accommodation has scissors, great! Mine doesn't. So, the fact I bought a pair with me has been a lifesaver. From opening milk and orange juice, to cutting loose threads, the uses for a pair of scissors are endless!!

5. Plenty of socks

Going to Spain I was thinking, no, I won't wear socks, I'll be in my flip flops or sandals all the time. How wrong was I! Contrary to popular believe, it does actually get a bit cold sometimes, so yes, socks are great for during the day, but also at night like bed socks.

Packing your case

The biggest piece of advice I can give you with regards to packing your case is check your case measurements and the weight of your case!

Particularly at the moment, RyanAir are changing their dimensions and weight restrictions every 5 minutes, so make sure you're aware of this so you don't incur any unexpected charges at the airport.

Also, make sure to pack your case properly. You will more than likely be taking a lot of stuff with you, so packing it properly will mean that you can get more in. Generally, shoes go at the bottom. If you have anything breakable or glass, it's often good to pop it inside one of your shoes as then it's less likely to break.

Another worry can be: what do I pack? What do I need? How can I survive 4 months with one case of stuff? What if I forget something important?

Don't worry! Below I have put 'draft' list of what you should or could take with you. This is my list for France, so it's designed for winter. Feel free to use it as a guide, as obviously everyone has different things they want to take with them, but this list should cover all the basics.

Checklist for Packing (FRANCE)

PANTS	14
SOCKS	12
BRAS	2 + WEAR ONE

TROUSERS	3 + WEAR ONE
JEANS	2
T-SHIRTS	
LONG SLEEVED TOPS	
JUMPERS	
GOING OUT TOPS	2
BOOTS	1
TRAINERS AND SANDALS	2
GYM GEAR	1
PYJAMAS	2/3
BIKINI & GOGGLES	
TOOTHBRUSH AND CHARGER AND HEAD	
TOOTHPASTE	
SHAMPOO	
HARIBRUSH	
HAIRCLIPS AND BOBBLES	
MAKE-UP AND COMPACT MIRROR	
HAND CREAM, HANDWASH	
DEODORANT, IMPULSE AND TED BAKER	
TAMPONS	
NAIL POLISH REMOVER	
FLANNEL	

JEWELLRY	
NAIL FILE AND VARNISH	
TOILET ROLL	
DENTAL FLOSS	
RAZORS	
BAG FOR UNI	
ALARM CLOCK	
DIARY	
YEAR ABROAD FORMS	
STATIONARY	
MINI SEWING KIT AND SCISSORS	
PASSPORT SIZED PICTURES AND PHOTOCOPIES	
SPARE GLASSES	
EAR PLUGS	
UMBRELLA	
USB	
KINDLE AND CHARGER	
PHONE AND CHARGER	
IPOD AND CHARGER	
LAPTOP AND CHARGER	
PLUGS	
MEDICATIONS	
SUNGLASSES	

TRAVEL KETTLE
TRAVEL IRON AND HAIRDRYER

Travelling as a student: discount cards, tips and advice

Remember, you may be on a Year Abroad, but you're still a student, which means you can benefit from student rates and discounts.

It's handy to have an International Student Identity Card, these come standard on the back of the NUS card (now known as TOTEM) and are perfect if anybody quibbles you being a student.

Also, there are special train passes for students, particularly in France, they have an 18-25 card, it's 50 euros, but with the pass you can get 30% off your trains. Which is definitely worth it if you plan on using the trains. If you're visiting another country you should check out if they offer a similar scheme.

If that wasn't enough, make sure to sign up to the loyalty cards. Cafes and supermarkets offer cards where you can collect points to get money off; or ones where if you buy 9 hot drinks, you get the 10th for free. As a student abroad, these are definitely worth making the most of, and you can also keep the cards as souvenirs.

Budgeting

Budgeting is important whilst you're away. You will receive your normal student finance from uni; be that loans or grants. On top of that, if you're travelling to an EU country, you will receive Erasmus funding.

Erasmus funding comes in two payments, the first at the start of your placement. This is 80% worth of your Erasmus funding and is only paid AFTER you have submitted your Certificate of Arrival; so make sure you have a bit of money before you leave for starting up costs, as in most cases it takes 1-2 weeks to receive your first payment.

The second payment is not until after your placement. This is the last 20%, and in some cases it can take up to a month to receive this, depending on when the holidays are. I remember that I received my last Spain payment on the same day as I got my first payment for France.

Because of this, it is very important to budget so you can keep track of how much you are spending and what you're spending it on.

I would also recommend that you calculate (approximately) how much funding in total you are expecting to receive over the year. That means that you can create a monthly amount, and say, I'll try not to spend more than ... per month. This way you won't have any financial difficulties. However, remember you will spend more money in your first month: on rent, buying food, setting everything up; you might need to buy things for your accommodation, or things you forgot, etc. So, try to give yourself a bigger budget for the first month.

The Erasmus forms

What forms are there?

There are quite a few forms...

Those of you on work placements will be pleased to discover that there are less forms. (but not by much!)

For work placements you just need to get the Learning Agreement filled out, and often and Insurance form. The only difficulty with these forms is encouraging your employer to fill in the necessary details, (which luckily for me, wasn't much of a problem.)

Then you only have the forms you do after your arrival, including:

-   Certificate of arrival: proves you are in the country doing what you said you were going to do
-   Confirmation of receiving your funding forms
-   End of placement employers report
-   Certificate of Attendance: proves you were there for the length of the placement

For studying it's a tiny bit more complex. This is because your original Learning Agreement is often subject to change. In the Studying Learning Agreement, you fill in details of the courses you wish to study which can change when you discover that: all of your subjects clash; one of your courses has been cancelled due to lack of interest or teacher illness, etc, or that the course you wanted to do is actually going to be really difficult and boring.

Therefore, you will generally have to fill out an Amended Learning Agreement.

Then you have:

- Certificate of Arrival
- Fulfilment of Learning Agreement (detailing your grades, and that you passed your courses)
- Certificate of Attendance
- Confirmation of receiving your funding forms

When you look at the list of them it doesn't look to bad. But don't forget that you also have the forms for the University itself.

These include:

- Accommodation forms
- Application to be a student at the university forms
- Signing up for French classes forms
- Applying for a student card

In France they had a form for everything. And quite often they'd be very good at losing these forms...

Assessments: grading systems in foreign countries in comparison with the UK

The table below shows the grade equivalents between the UK, France, Italy, Germany, the Netherlands and Spain, so that you can understand what your grades mean.

UK Ireland	Italy	France Belgium	Germany Austria (Some universities use a point system instead)	Netherlands	Spain
75+	30L	18-20	1+	10	9,5
70	30	16	1	9	9
67	29	14	1-	8,5	8,5
64	28	13	2+	8	8
61	27	12	2	7,5	7,5
58	26	11.5	2-	7	7
55	25	11.5	3+	6,9	6,5
52	24	11	3	6,7	6,3
50	23	11	3-	6,6	6,1
48	22	10.5	4+	6,5	5,9
46	21	10.5	4	6,4	5,7
44	20	10	4	6,2	5,5
42	19	10	4	6,1	5,3
40	18	10	4	6	5

Assessments from your home university: examples from my uni

Every university has different assessments that you have to complete whilst on your Year Abroad. In this section I will explain the assessment system at my university: Portsmouth. Please note this information is correct as of 2017/8 but may change for other year groups.

The system at Portsmouth is comprised of 3 main parts:

- The risk assessment
- An online tutorial
- The Year Abroad Report

The risk assessment is very quick and simple. It's just a quick online document where you put information such as the country you're going to; the phone number for the embassy (just in case) and where you read security an health information about your chosen country. This ensures you have some knowledge about the country you are visiting before you get there. It maybe isn't too important for most European countries, as there are a lot of similarities, but for Asian countries or African countries, that have such different systems and life styles, it's good to know what to expect.

Then halfway through your placement you have to complete an online tutorial. This is another online document where you answer basic questions like how you are getting on; what's your accommodation like; do you have a good work/life or study/life balance, etc. If you have any issues this is a good time to mention them, so your tutor is aware and can help you out.

The final part of the assessment is the Year Abroad Report. This is the bit that actually counts. You have to write 3000 words (or 1,500 if you visited two countries as there will be one for each country) in the target language. This report is what they use to ensure you have the correct level to proceed to the next year, so use it as a chance to show off your new language skills. More importantly, you have complete freedom on the topic of your report, so you can write about whatever part of your time abroad interested you most.

How to cope with culture shock

Coping with culture shock can be difficult. You've just moved to a foreign country; you're all alone, it's not the easiest thing to adjust to.

I think the best piece of advice I could give to someone going on a Year Abroad is not to have any expectations. The Spanish have a siesta every day, so all the shops are closed from 2 until 5. Ok, unexpected but fair enough. The French people keep staring at me and making me feel uncomfortable. Weird, but I guess that's how they do it here. Try not to get irritated by these differences, instead try to embrace them. Have a go at having a siesta or trying the local food no matter how weird it sounds. And make friends with the natives. The more native friends you have; the more you'll start to understand why they do things the way that they do.

Keeping a record of your Year Abroad

A Year Abroad is one of those things you only ever do once, so it's important to keep a record of it, so you never forget it. You could do this by taking pictures to put in an album or scrapbook, writing a blog (or book), doing a video diary or collecting small momentos like napkins from restaurants or cafes you've visited.

Working in Spain

Most importantly, for working anywhere: Research the company before you go. This way you know that the company and the job you'll be doing is what you're expecting and also that the job is legit.

Ensure the company don't take advantage of you. For instance: I didn't get paid for my work in Spain. But I only generally worked 16 hours a week and I got free Spanish lessons.

Bearing this in mind, you need to work hard. Yes, it is a year for enjoying yourself and experiencing new things, but you need to get something from it, i.e good experience working in a certain sector; improving your linguistic abilities. Because at the end of the day, the Year Abroad is about improving your language skills so you'll be at the correct level for the last year of uni.

Studying Abroad:

ESN trips

The ESN is the Erasmus Student Network. This network runs in a variety of different universities across Europe. They run lots of trips and events to enable Erasmus students to make the most of their year, but also have the chance to experience the culture and meet new people. If you happen to be at a uni which offers these trips: Go for it! Make the most of these trips! They are all subsidised, so they work out a lot cheaper than if you decided to do it by yourself and it's a great way of making friends too.

Courses

There are so many courses on offer it can be difficult to know what to pick. Universities have different requirements, but my university just said: You can do whatever you want as long as it's taught in French. (I.e.: you can't pick courses taught in English) which was fair enough, I wasn't there to practise my English.

What is on offer:

Generally the uni will have an online database where you can view all the courses on offer. These range from literature, history, science, law to things like sport, performing arts and learning new languages.

I would recommend that you choose a mixture of courses. Definitely pick the language courses. These will help you continue to practise your language skills in a non-judgemental environment. And if they have a Tandem scheme: go for it. It'll massively improve both your level and confidence.

As for the rest of you choices: if you're interested in translation or interpreting, it's a good idea to pick these. The extra experience will stand you in good stead for the final year. Just pay attention to how they do their exams: are you allowed a dictionary for translation? What level is the course? If it's designed for Native students you are very likely to struggle, so go for the ones designed for exchange students as they're not quite so picky with their marking on these ones.

What is your dissertation about? If you're writing a dissertation on German Music and Folklore (a random example), and they offer a class called German Music and Folklore- pick it, it'll be useful for your dissertation.

For the others; consider trying something new. I decided to try some literature classes and Beginners Italian. These were completely different for me: the last time I'd studied literature was back in secondary school (and that was only English Literature!) and I didn't know a word of Italian asides from Ciao Bella!

At the end of the day, pick whatever you want. You are the one who is going to have to study it for the next half a year or whole year, so pick wisely. Pick things you're interested in and then you won't find it hard to stay motivated.

Accommodation

Finding accommodation can be a challenge. I was very lucky, I got a place in halls in France. (Well I say I was lucky:

the accommodation was fine but the amount of forms I had to fill out was unbelievable!)

On one hand halls is easier, because you haven't got to worry about being kicked out if a landlord decides not to rent to you anymore and you aren't likely to get a dodgy landlord or end up living in a dump.

However, in some places it is hard to get into halls; take Ronda for instance. When I was in Spain I couldn't stay in halls; I was working and there wasn't a uni in Ronda.

In this case I'd suggest looking online. There are a range of websites where you can find adverts with people renting rooms out. Also you should join the neighbourhood groups, this way you can get local recommendations from the natives who know the area best.

And if worst comes to worst, get a hotel for the first week and look for something when you get there. Your employer or university will be able to help you and you'll be able to view first hand where you'll be living before you sign on the dotted line.

Another option is living with a family. If you're someone who's uncertain of living on your own: cooking for yourself, be responsible for everything. Consider living with a family. Although this can limit your freedom, as you need to respect the other family members, so preferably you shouldn't be out late every night. It will give you a unique experience and you will be practising your language skills 24/7! And after a long day working or studying you'll have the advantage of coming home to (hopefully) nice people and a home cooked meal.

Printed in Poland
by Amazon Fulfillment
Poland Sp. z o.o., Wrocław